Stories for Classroom and Assembly

The importance of developing children's personal, spiritual, emotional and moral education has become a key inclusion in the modern school curriculum. Yet, for the busy primary school teacher, integrating values education into the average school day is a tricky and time-consuming task, and one that can too easily be neglected.

This book is an indispensable resource for use in both the classroom and assembly, providing a delightful collection of fifteen original themed stories and activities, designed to develop key values and skills.

Using the power of story, it stimulates reflection and discussion on a range of topics. The material is presented to maximise fun in learning, flexibility, and coverage of National Curriculum guidelines for values education teaching. Amongst key values discussed are:

- personal responsibility and independence
- cooperation and sharing
- honesty and justice
- respect for world religions.

Each session contributes to key skills in English, whilst many of the activities involve use of coordination, numeracy and science skills. In addition, the stories are implicitly multi-cultural in flavour, giving a diverse and yet inclusive feel to the book as a whole.

Teachers at Key Stages 1 and 2, student teachers, headteachers, and literacy co-ordinators alike, will find this book an irresistably charming, and yet practical tool. Its topical tales and photocopiable resources make it an essential classroom companion.

Professor Mal Leicester is Chair of Learning and Teaching at Nottingham University.

Stories for Classroom and Assembly

Active learning in values education at
Key Stages One and Two

Mal Leicester

rf RoutledgeFalmer
Taylor & Francis Group

LONDON AND NEW YORK

First published 2003
by RoutledgeFalmer
11 New Fetter Lane, London EC4P 4EE

Simultaneously published in the USA and Canada
by RoutledgeFalmer
29 West 35th Street, New York, NY 10001

RoutledgeFalmer is an imprint of
the Taylor & Francis Group

© 2003 Mal Leicester

Typeset in Times New Roman by GreenGate Publishing Services,
Tonbridge, Kent
Printed and bound in Great Britain by TJ International Ltd,
Padstow, Cornwall

British Library Cataloguing in Publication Data
A catalogue record for this book is available from the British
Library

Library of Congress Cataloging in Publication Data
A catalog record has been requested

ISBN 0–415–28699–9

Contents

Acknowledgements

I wish to express my appreciation to the University Writers' Circle for helpful comments on these stories. I am also very grateful to Gill Johnson for advice about the suitability of the vocabulary and activities for Key Stage One. As always, I received inspiration from my daughter, Jane Dover. Finally, warm thanks to Karen Langley who not only typed the manuscript, but with her invariable efficiency and kindness, supported its production in many ways.

Mal Leicester

Introduction

Story in education

Story and learning

Story telling has always been a powerful and basic human activity. In all civilisations and cultures, both the activity of story telling and significant, individual stories have been passed down the generations. This is because, long before the printed word was available, story was the means by which people attempted to make sense of their experience of the world, to communicate that understanding and to achieve a collective wisdom through passing on accumulating knowledge and values in a memorable and accessible way.

Story telling has thus not only entertained us, providing consolation and escape from the tedious, often painful burden of everyday 'real' life, it has also been part of our collective construction of knowledge. Think of each story as a fragment of truth, each one adding to our understanding of the human condition. Cumulatively, stories add to our understanding of the complexity and diversity of human motivation and relations, enabling us to glimpse universal truths in the unending particularity of context and situation. Thus stories simultaneously *educate* and *entertain*. Through story, *learning is fun*.

Children feel this dual power of story. They readily engage with stories of all kinds. Think of your own childhood. Certainly I can vividly remember, in my own early childhood, my grandmother's stories about 'the olden days'; that almost unimaginable time when my parents were young – or even not yet born. And then with my developing love of books I discovered favourites which I will always remember with affection – lifelong treasures: *The Enchanted Wood*; *Winnie The Pooh*; *William Brown*; *Little Women* and so on. To use this love of story in early education makes sense. It gives teachers a powerful pedagogical tool. Not only can children make sense of their own experience through telling their own stories, listening to stories will stimulate their thinking, encourage discussion and cooperative activity, reveal a variety of points of view, encourage self-knowledge and teach them about the world in which they live. Perhaps above all, stories introduce children to the complex, fascinating and important realm of *values*.

Story, values and education

In his book *On Stories*, Richard Kearney discusses the five-part Aristotelian model for narrative: plot, re-creation, release (catharsis), wisdom and ethics. In his discussion he notes the power of empathy in fiction and quotes Richard Rorty as follows:

narratives not only help to humanise aliens, strangers and scapegoats – as Harriet Beecher Stowe's *Uncle Tom's Cabin* did, for example, regarding white prejudices against blacks – but also to make each one of us into an 'agent of love' sensitive to the particular details of others' pain and humiliation.

Kearney also points out that stories are never neutral; each carries an evaluative charge.

What better tool than stories, then, for values education? The development of such an emotionally, morally and spiritually fundamental quality as 'empathy' is intrinsic to engagement with story, and particular stories will inevitably introduce a whole range of values. Moreover, stories encapsulate value issues, stimulating reflection and discussion about conflicts of values and moral dilemmas.

The National Curriculum requires the development of personal, social, moral, emotional, cultural and spiritual values. Thus it recognises that as well as the distinctively educational values of rationality and criticality, there are various other kinds of educationally relevant values too. We must not simply educate minds, attending only to a child's cognitive development, we must educate character, emotion, imagination and spirit. In other words, education is of the whole child and this holistic conception of educational development is in keeping with developing values as an integral part of the whole curriculum.

It has long been recognised, too, that values are always implicit in what we teach and how we teach it. It is important, therefore, to learn to scrutinise those implicit values, and to choose wisely those values that we implicitly endorse (in story as well as in teaching approach, for example) in addition to those we explicitly encourage. The stories and learning activities in this book focus, implicitly and explicitly, on worthwhile values in personal, social, moral, emotional and spiritual education.

Thus, because as a teacher you are charged with developing values across the curriculum, this book seeks to help you to use stories to do just that, and to do it in an enjoyable way. (Children must, almost above all, learn to love learning!) With this resource, the development of personal, social, moral, emotional and spiritual values becomes an integral part of your classroom activities. You need no longer be anxious that you may be neglecting values education, since alongside the development of key skills, particularly literacy-related skills, fifteen stories and associated activities are structured to encourage the understanding and development of fifteen key values.

How to use the book

Fifteen new stories are grouped into three sets; each set includes one theme from each of *five aspects* of values education: personal, social, emotional, moral and spiritual. Thus each aspect covers three key values as follows:

Aspect of values education	Key values
1 Personal	(i) Personal Responsibility (ii) Independence (iii) Self-confidence
2 Social	(i) Cooperation (ii) Sharing (iii) Friendship

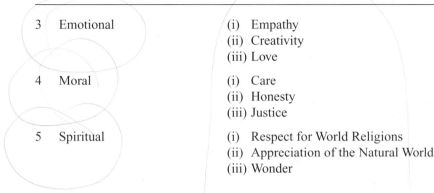

3	Emotional	(i) Empathy
		(ii) Creativity
		(iii) Love
4	Moral	(i) Care
		(ii) Honesty
		(iii) Justice
5	Spiritual	(i) Respect for World Religions
		(ii) Appreciation of the Natural World
		(iii) Wonder

Flexibility

Each of these fifteen key values is the focus for one teaching session. These fifteen sessions should be used to suit your teaching schedule. For example, you could use one session per week for fifteen weeks. Each session provides a story, some points for discussion and follow-up associated educational activities. Though approximate times are suggested for these activities, obviously you should set a pace which suits you and your class.

The intention is to save you time by providing good values material for classroom work and for the school assembly, but you can be flexible in how you use this material. For instance, you may prefer a different sequence – perhaps because some of the later stories link with work you are currently doing and therefore could be used first.

The sessions

- Having introduced the theme of the story you can tell *or* read it.

- The children could sit in a circle for the story and discussion time.

- Deal with 'difficult' vocabulary in your usual way. This is often to explain words as you come to them in the story.

- You may or may not want to ask the *closed* (comprehension-type) questions to check understanding. You may want to ask some of them as you read or only after you have finished reading, or not at all.

- You can select or add to the more *open* 'points for discussion' – according to those aspects of the theme most relevant to your curriculum.

- You can select or add to the suggested activities. Some activities could be used in follow-up lessons.

- You may wish to use the classroom activity partly as preparation for the relevant assembly. Suggestions are given.

- Also for the assembly, suggested poems and songs are given. The suggestions are taken from commonly used texts. However, should you have different poetry and song books in your school, you will find that it is not difficult to find poems and songs which are relevant to the themes.

- You can involve the children as active participants in the assembly to different degrees, commensurate with the custom in your school.

- You can link the themes with each other and with other on-going projects. For example, themes ten (Appreciation of the Natural World) and fifteen (Wonder at Creation) would link well with environmental education; themes one (Personal Responsibility), two (Cooperation), four (Honesty and Trust), nine (Kindness and Care) and fourteen (Justice) with citizenship education; and theme five (Respect for World Religions) with multi-faith religious education.

The curriculum

You will find that as well as having a particular focus on values education, each session contributes to key skills in English (as you would expect, given the valuing of story). Thus each session involves such skills as listening, talking, reflecting, reasoning and concentrating. Many of the activities also develop coordination skills and art and craft work, some highlight numeracy and several focus on aspects of science. In addition, the stories make an implicit contribution to multicultural education. They contain children of various ethnic origins and embody respect for diversity. Stories, discussion and activities all have regard to the stimulation of critical thought *and* the stimulation of the imagination.

Age levels

The material is intended for use at Key Stages One and Two. Since these stages include a relatively wide age range (4–10 years) you will obviously use the material at the developmental level appropriate for your children. Thus a class of younger children will 'tell' rather than 'write' their own stories and learn to recognise key words. Older children, on the other hand, will be able to write their own associated stories and poems and may even take a turn in reading part of the theme story in classroom or assembly.

Precious time

The book is intended to be a useful and *time-saving* resource for classroom and assembly. I am sure that, like all learning/teaching resources, it will be used in a whole variety of different ways. Some teachers may reach for the book as the basis for a morning's work on those (rare but inevitable!) occasions when they have simply not had time to prepare material of their own (or it may be their turn to prepare an assembly). Other teachers may take each story/activity as the starting point for an extended project on the highlighted theme. Some schools may use the book as the basis for a whole school approach to values education and some may wish to encourage parents to use the book to work with their child. It could provide bedtime or rainy-day stories with the bonus of discussion points and associated educational activities. In whatever way you choose to use it, I hope that you and the children will enjoy the theme stories and the activities and that these will genuinely promote the development of those worthwhile values which should be part of a balanced education.

Chapter 1

Story Book Dream

Teacher's Notes

Theme One: The value of **Personal Responsibility**

Values Education: Learning to be responsible is part of **Personal Education**

All day and every day schools guide children towards responsible behaviour. The idea of 'personal responsibility' is usually implicit. This story provides an opportunity for the children to focus explicitly on 'personal responsibility' and to explore it with their teacher.

Lesson Plan

This five-part lesson plan is only a guide. Teachers are likely to add to or amend the learning activities which are suggested and may sometimes wish to substitute their own. For any part of the session they may wish to allow more or less time than that suggested.

1 Introduce the theme   *5–10 minutes*

What is **responsibility**?
The teacher gives examples and explains why we should be responsible.
The teacher can link this to 'trust'. The children add some examples of their own and talk about these.

2 Vocabulary   *5 minutes*

The teacher ensures that the children understand the words given.
This can be integrated into the reading of the story.

3 The story   *5–10 minutes*

The teacher shows the illustration and reads the story.

4 Talking about the story   *10–15 minutes*

The teacher uses some of the questions and discussion points given, stimulating the children to talk about the story/theme. Some of the questions could be integrated into the reading of the story.

5 The learning activity   *20–35 minutes*

Selecting a book/the telling of stories/making a bookmark.
Some suggested activities could be used in subsequent, follow-up lessons.

| Total time | *45–75 minutes* |

1 INTRODUCE THE THEME

Key points

● The concept of 'personal responsibility' is a difficult one for a child to understand.

● The teacher should try to convey that to be responsible is to be sensible *and* reliable *and* fair, and that we can *trust* people who are responsible.

● Give examples such as looking out for the safety of younger children, not being too rough with other children or objects, not scribbling on books, keeping your promise, etc.

● Lead the children into giving some examples of their own and talk with the class about these.

2 VOCABULARY

Use your usual methods for introducing new words.

The difficult words in the story are:

responsible	-	*sensible/reliable/accountable/making sensible decisions for yourself*
glossy	-	*shiny*
shrill voice	-	*a high-pitched and piercing voice*
disappointed/disappointment	-	*lost hope/saddened by the failure of an expectation or want*
every nook and cranny	-	*every little space*
confess	-	*own up*
slam	-	*bang*
eager	-	*keen*
vivid	-	*strong, bright colour and detail*
tumbled	-	*fell down*

Story Book Dream

Grace has accepted responsibility for her library book

Story Book Dream

Grace loved stories. Whenever she had a new book she would hold it for a moment, enjoying the picture on the cover, and once she began to read, she was lost to the world. One day at school, Mrs Cavanagh, the teacher, said that Grace's class could have a library lesson. In the library she gave each child a library card.

"Everyone can choose a book to take home. You must bring it back in two weeks," she said.

Grace went straight to the shelves of story books. She found exciting adventure books, adventurous school stories and magical tales. She was spoiled for choice.

"Hurry up Grace," said Mrs Cavanagh. She sounded quite sharp. "Everyone else is reading already."

Quickly Grace chose a thin book with the picture of a black princess on the cover. It was called *The Black Rose*. The princess was beautiful and the cover was glossy.

As Grace began to read she was so gripped by the story that the school library faded from her mind and she jumped when Mrs Cavanagh's shrill voice drilled into her left ear.

"I – said – close – your – book."

Grace shot up straight, closing her book at once. She saw that the other children were looking at her, some with a smirk. They must all have been watching as Mrs Cavanagh had crept up on her.

"Now Grace," said the teacher, "you're such a dilly-daydream, please don't lose that book."

That night Grace enjoyed reading her book in bed. She wanted to know what happened in the end but before she could find out her mum came in and said, "Lights out Grace. Time to sleep now." Disappointed, Grace placed the book in the empty drawer of her bedside cabinet, snapping this closed with a cross thud, before she snuggled down, to think about the princess in her palace far away.

At bedtime the next day, Grace changed into her pyjamas extra quickly, eager to find out what happened next in the story. But when she opened the drawer to take out the book, she had a shock. An empty drawer stared back at her. The book had gone.

"Mum," she shouted. Her mum came to see what the matter was.

"You must have moved it somewhere else and forgotten," she said. "We'll find it tomorrow."

But though Grace and her mum searched and searched, first in every nook and cranny of Grace's bedroom, and then all over the rest of the house, the book had completely disappeared.

"You're responsible for that book, Grace. You should have taken more care."

"I know mum. I thought I had. I'm sure I put it in the drawer."

"Well it can't have moved by itself," said mum crossly. "You're in a daydream half the time."

Every day for two weeks Grace searched for the book. Several times she opened the drawer, unable to believe that the book really wasn't there. As she began to lose all hope of finding it, she became more and more worried. How could she confess to Mrs Cavanagh, who would be very angry? Each morning, as the days marched relentlessly by, she looked anxiously at the kitchen calendar. Grace was dreading the day she was supposed to take back the book.

The day before the dreaded library day, she still hadn't found it.

"I will pay for it mum," she said. "Out of my pocket money. However long it takes."

"Well yes, so you should," mum agreed.

That night it took ages for Grace to get to sleep. She tossed and turned, sick with dread about having to confess to Mrs Cavanagh. When at last she did fall asleep, she had a particularly vivid dream. She dreamed that she fell off a high cliff, and as she tumbled towards the ground, she actually turned into a book. Her pages fluttered open like paper wings. She landed with a thud, but unhurt, onto black sand. Crashing waves were shouting, "find me, find me." The waves were coming nearer and nearer. The book couldn't move. She would get soaking wet and drown. It was very frightening. Fortunately, just as a huge, green wave towered above her, poised to crash down, she woke up.

She lay in her warm, safe, dry bed thinking about her dream. A falling, flying book!

Grace had a strange feeling. It was the feeling she had when a word she had forgotten was on the tip of her tongue.

"What am I trying to remember?" she wondered.

Into her mind came the sound of the dream thud as she, the dream book, had landed on the beach. Suddenly she remembered the real thud of the drawer when she had slammed it shut on the real book.

"I did put it in there," she thought. "I did."

In the darkness Grace leaned over and opened the drawer of her bedside cabinet. She felt inside, pushing her hand right to the back. Her heart gave a leap of surprise. There was no wooden back to the drawer. She felt a gap at the back of the cabinet. Grace jumped out of bed and switched on the light. Kneeling in front of the cabinet she took out the drawer. She stretched her arm into the space and her hand was just small enough to squeeze down into the gap at the back. With the tips of her fingers she could feel something there. She managed to grasp the edge of this object and to pull it up to the top and out. She gazed down in delight. There it was, her book. The beautiful princess, undamaged, was smiling up at her. Grace hugged the book to her chest, closing her eyes in a thrill of relief. She felt like whooping with joy, but it was the silent middle of the night. Instead she got back into bed, found her place in the book and read on to the end. She finished as the birds began to sing with the dawn. Only then did Grace fall fast asleep.

Surprisingly, she wasn't tired when her mum woke her for school. She was too eager to tell her about finding the book. And, of course, with the book found, she was now really looking forward to the library lesson. She could swap *The Black Rose* for another adventurous story.

4 TALKING ABOUT THE STORY

Did the children understand?

- What happened whenever Grace began to read?

- What was the title of the book Grace chose?

- Did Grace put the book in the drawer?

- Why did the dream make her look once more in the drawer?

- Where had the book gone?

Points for discussion

- Had Grace been responsible about where she put her book?
  (We can be responsible and still things can go wrong.)

- How did she show responsibility when the book went missing?
  (Searching, planning to pay for it.)

- Why should we be responsible for our library books?
  (Others want to read them too. We are trusted with them.)

- Why do we like stories?
  (We learn in an enjoyable way.)

- In addition, you could use this opportunity to explore, with the children, the difference between fiction and reality.

5 THE LEARNING ACTIVITY

Links

i)   The activity links with the story through book selection and story telling.

ii) The assembly connects with the story through valuing responsibility and valuing books and stories.

iii) If you wish to link the activity to the assembly, when the children are telling their stories, listen for a particularly appropriate one, told by a confident child. This could then be retold by the child in the follow-up assembly. Alternatively, a child could rehearse the poem *Enter Adventure*.

ACTIVITY SUGGESTIONS

- These activities involve working as individuals, in pairs and as a whole class.
- The children will need: (1) a library or book box (2) thin card, crayons or stick-on shapes.

1 BOOK TIME

Allow the children to select a book (from the class library corner, book box or school library).

Allow the children a few quiet minutes for looking at the book they have chosen.

Encourage the children to explain to you why they chose that book. What did they like about it? This could be done directly to you when they are looking at their books, or with the children in a circle, told to the whole class, afterwards.

2 STORY TIME

Ask the children to remember a dream they have had. In pairs, the children tell each other their dream.

Ask each child to remember when they or someone they know lost something. What was it? Did it get found? Again the children talk about this in pairs.

Some of the children could tell the whole class their dream or their lost and found story.

And/or draw a picture from one part of their dream or story and write about what is happening.

3 MAKING A BOOKMARK

Cut a length of thin card for each child. You could stamp a hole in the top of each and the children could thread thin ribbon through this – good practice for coordination skills and for tying a knot or bow.

Using paint, crayons, coloured pens or stick-on coloured shapes, the children decorate their own bookmark. Older children could write "BOOKMARK" on one side and their name on the other, and decorate in and around the letters.

Assembly

Theme: **Personal Responsibility**

Introduction

The assembly leader introduces the theme and talks about why we should be responsible in how we behave. (How could we trust people if they were not reliable?) Give examples of reliable/responsible people. Give examples of how the children can be responsible.

Story

A child could read this poem to introduce the story (optional)

Enter Adventure

Come in and welcome
To a world full of glory,
Enter Adventure
I'll tell you a story.
Of love and laughter, horror and fright
Of good against evil
The age-old fight.
Peace and quiet, sound and fury
Enter adventure
I'll tell you a story.

Assembly leader:

"Our story today is about Grace, a girl who loved stories and who was very responsible about her story book. In a sense, dreams, like stories, are not real, but it was a dream that helped Grace to find her real book."

The assembly leader reads the story – *Story Book Dream.*

And/or:

A child tells their 'lost and found' story.

Poem or song

You can choose a poem or a song or both. Select poems and songs which are relevant to the theme or which echo the story in some way.

Examples

Poems:

Excuses (the excuses we make when we have not been responsible!)
Page 61 in *Please Mrs Butler* by Allan Ahlberg, published by Puffin,1984.

What I Like (love of reading books)
Page 85 in *Smile Please* by Tony Bradman, published by Puffin, 1989.

Songs:

When a Knight Won His Spurs (reflects 'storyland' and personal virtue)
No. 34 in *Someone's Singing Lord* (2nd edition), published by A&C Black, 2002.
An amusing poem about this song is 'Headmaster's Hymn,' Page 28 in *Please Mrs Butler* by Allan Ahlberg, published by Puffin,1984.

A Better World (echoes of waking up and living well – responsible living)
No. 60 in *Alleluya* (2nd edition), published by A&C Black, 1980.

Such Hard Work (being responsible and kind is hard work)
No. 29 in *Every Colour Under the Sun*, published by Ward Lock Educational Co. Ltd., 1983.

Quiet reflection or prayer

For a universal, humanistic or multi-faith assembly:

Quiet reflection

The assembly leader says:
"Think for a moment of what a muddle we would be in if no one could be relied on. We would not get up in time for school. Your teacher would not be here. No one would meet you at home time. (Pause) Let us feel grateful that people are responsible towards us. Let us feel grateful to those people we can trust. (Pause) We can all try to be sensible and reliable and helpful. We can all try to be worthy of trust. Think about how you can be more responsible today." (Pause)

Or for Christian schools:

Prayer

Let us pray.

Dear God,
Thank you for all the people we can trust: those who care for us, those who teach us, those who play with us. Help us to be trustworthy too. Help us to be sensible and reliable and helpful today. Almighty God, we place our trust in you.
Amen.

Chapter 2

The Bumblebee Man

Teacher's Notes

Theme Two: The value of **Cooperation**

Values Education: Learning to cooperate is part of **Social Education**

> Children cooperate all the time but may not have thought about it or recognised its importance as a valuable part of friendly, social relations.

Lesson Plan

This five-part lesson plan is only a guide. Teachers are likely to add to or amend the learning activities which are suggested and may sometimes wish to substitute their own. For any part of the session they may wish to allow more or less time than that suggested.

1 Introduce the theme *5–10 minutes*

What is **cooperation**?
The teacher gives examples and explains why we should cooperate.
The children add some examples of their own and talk about these.

2 Vocabulary *5 minutes*

The teacher ensures that the children understand the words given.
This can be integrated into the reading of the story.

3 The story *5–10 minutes*

The teacher shows the illustration and reads the story.

4 Talking about the story *10–15 minutes*

The teacher uses some of the questions and discussion points given, stimulating the children to talk about the story/theme.
Some of the questions could be integrated into the reading of the story.

5 The learning activity *20–35 minutes*

The class cooperates in constructing a class painting/shopping.
Some suggested activities could be used in subsequent, follow-up lessons.

Total time | *45–75 minutes*

INTRODUCE THE THEME

Key points

- The concept of 'cooperation' overlaps with, but is distinct from, the concept of helping.

- The teacher should explain that we cooperate when we help *each other* by doing something *together*.

- Give examples such as working in pairs in the class, or washing and drying-up dishes with someone, or holding down the paper on a parcel while the other person sticks on the sticky tape etc.

- Lead the children into giving some examples of their own and talk with the class about these.

VOCABULARY

Use your usual methods for introducing new words.

The difficult words in the story are:

cooperation	-	*working helpfully with another; joint action*
example	-	*an instance which explains an idea; a model or sample or illustration*
pedestrian	-	*someone who walks to a place*
pedestrianised	-	*made for walking (instead of driving) down*
indignant	-	*angry and scornful at injustice or wrong-doing*
tantrum	-	*the out-of-control rage of a young child*
statue	-	*a large stone, wood or plastic figure (sculpture) of a person or animal*
rescued	-	*saved*

3 THE STORY:

The Bumblebee Man

Mollie and Maosen cooperate in finding Jie's mummy

The Bumblebee Man

"**W**ell Mollie, and what do *you* think it means?" asked Mrs Cooke.

Mollie jumped. She had been lost in a dream.

"I'm sorry Mrs Cooke," she said. "What does what mean?"

"I thought you weren't paying attention," said her teacher. "I could do with a little *cooperation* my dear." Mrs Cooke emphasised the word 'cooperation' and to Mollie's surprise, this made the children laugh.

"Cooperation," repeated Mrs Cooke. "What does it mean?"

"Helping someone to do something," said Mollie.

"A good try dear," said Mrs Cooke. "When two people cooperate they certainly do help each other to do something they both want done. It's not just one helping the other though. Who can give me an example?"

"I went on an errand for my mum," said Susie.

"That was a good thing to do Susie," said Mrs Cooke. "That was helping your mum. Just one helper. What about cooperation though?"

"My dad planted a small tree in our garden and I held it straight while he put on the soil and patted it down," said Adam.

"Good," said Mrs Cooke. "You and your dad cooperated in planting that tree. You both helped. It needed you both didn't it? What else?"

There was a long silence. Mollie tried hard to think of something to make up for not listening before, but her mind was a blank. Maosen, her friend, was frowning with effort. It was harder for him because his family had moved to Beeston in England from China, and he was still learning English as fast as he could.

"Well, everyone," said Mrs Cooke. "Think hard over the weekend. I want examples on Monday. Especially from you Mollie. And your own ideas please children. No asking your mum."

That Saturday Mollie and Maosen were in Mollie's garden, breaking bread for the birds. Maosen was tossing big white chunks onto the green grass while Mollie scattered tiny pieces over the square, flat top of the bird table. A bee buzzed by Mollie's ear and landed on Maosen's outstretched hand.

"Keep still Maosen," said Mollie, "or it might sting."

Maosen held his hand very still. Hardly daring to breath, the children watched as the bee walked a few inches across Maosen's skin before flying away. Maosen breathed a sigh of relief.

"What's the name of that?" he asked.

"Bumblebee," said Mollie.

It was a hard word to say. Maosen had to practise several times.

"Bumblebee, Bumblebee, Bumblebee. I like that name," he said.

"Me too," said Mollie. "A fuzzy, wuzzy bumblebee."

"Like a fly in a fur coat," Maosen said, which made Mollie laugh.

"Mollie," her mum called from the kitchen window, "I can hear you're enjoying yourselves, but would you go on an errand please? We're out of milk."

Mollie liked going to the shops for her mum – along the pedestrianised High Street, the brown basket over her arm. She and Maosen went together. Maosen found it interesting to go into English shops and always asked Mollie the names of lots of things which Mollie enjoyed telling him.

That day he learned doughnut and sausage, and, startled by the indignant rage of a toddler, he learned 'tantrum' too.

"Tantrum," he repeated. "Very loud," he added, disapprovingly.

Eventually Mollie and Maosen came out of the big store, their carton of milk in their basket, and began to walk back towards the High Street. Halfway there they saw another small child in tears, but this one was not having a tantrum, she was heartbroken. She was shaking with sobs, tears of grief streaming down her tiny face. Mollie felt very sorry for her. The child was repeating a word which Mollie couldn't understand. Maosen could though. By coincidence, the little girl was Chinese.

"She's calling for her mummy," Maosen told Mollie.

Maosen spoke to her in Chinese. He spoke very kindly and the child began to calm down.

"She's lost," Maosen explained.

"Ask her where she lost her mummy," Mollie suggested. She watched as Maosen spoke to the child. He laughed at her reply.

"She said she was by the bumblebee man," he said to Mollie. "Whatever can she mean?"

"I know!" exclaimed Mollie. "Come." She took the child's hand and hurried on towards the High Street.

"The statue round the corner," she explained to Maosen, "he's got huge stone bumblebees on his hat."

As they rounded the corner Mollie saw near the statue a worried Chinese woman looking up and down the street. Her face lit up when she saw them.

"Jie," she called.

Little Jie ran towards her mummy and flew into her arms.

As Mollie and Maosen followed more slowly, the little girl pointed at them, chatting rapidly.

"Thank you," the woman said to them. "Thank you so very much. But how did you find me?"

"Maosen could talk with her," Mollie explained. "He's Chinese like you, and I knew what she meant by the 'bumblebee man'."

"What a splendid cooperation!" said Jie's mum, in excellent English.

Mollie and Maosen smiled at each other. Not only had they rescued Jie, about which they were very pleased, they had, they realised, found a true example, for their teacher, of a splendid cooperation indeed.

4 TALKING ABOUT THE STORY

Did the children understand?

- For what word did Mrs Cook ask the children to think of an example?

- How did Adam cooperate with his dad?

- In the garden, why did Mollie tell Maosen to keep his hand still?

- What did Mollie have to buy at the shops?

- Why was Jie crying?

- Where was Jie's mummy?

Points for discussion

- Why is it good to cooperate with each other?
  (Some tasks need more than one person. Cooperation builds good relationships/friendships.)

- Why was finding an example harder for Maosen?
  (The teacher talks about learning a language and also a second language. Some children in the class may be bilingual. This is an opportunity for those children to show their skill. What is the word in _____ [name their language] for garden, milk, meat, girl, lost, etc.)

- Why did rescuing Jie need both Mollie and Maosen?
  (This brings in the idea of translation. This in turn introduces the difficult idea of *meaning* of words. Language is social. A conversation involves cooperation.)

- What should we do if we get lost?
  (This gives the teacher the opportunity to explain 'stranger' and to suggest that Jie could go to a woman at the cash till in the big store – not to a stranger in the street or in a small shop. What to do, not do, etc.)

5 THE LEARNING ACTIVITY

Links

i)   The activity links with the story through taking the form of a cooperative project.

ii) The assembly connects with the story through valuing cooperation.

iii) If you wish to link the activity to the assembly, pin up the children's 'High Street' in the assembly hall.

ACTIVITY SUGGESTIONS

- These activities involve working in pairs and as a whole class.

- The children will need: **1** drawing paper, and pens, paint or crayons, Blue-tac or drawing pins **2** 'toy' money.

1   THE HIGH STREET FRIEZE

The activity involves working in pairs towards a whole-class project. The children should understand that they are cooperating with their partner to produce a joint part of the class frieze. The class will finish up with a long picture of a busy shopping street.

Divide the children into pairs. Give each pair a large piece of paper. Each pair has to do a picture of a different shop (a book shop, toy shop, shoe shop, bakers, etc.) with different people walking by or looking in the window (a mother with a baby, a young boy with a dog, a man in a wheelchair, etc.). Crayons, coloured pencils or paint can be used.

When all the pictures are finished, they should be pinned in a long line, on the wall, to make up **The High Street**. A whole-class cooperation in making a frieze.

2   SHOPPING

For some related maths work, the children could take it in turns to be shopkeeper and shopper in one of **The High Street** shops – as the shopper, the children pay for items they ask for. As the shopkeeper, the children give the correct change.

Assembly

Theme: Cooperation

Introduction

The assembly leader introduces the theme and talks about why and how we cooperate together. S/he gives examples of ways in which the children cooperate.

Story

Assembly leader:

"Our story today is about two children who cooperate in doing something important. Cooperation is a bit like a conversation, you take it in turns – one to listen and one to speak. It is because of Maosen, that Mollie and Maosen are able to do their important thing."

The assembly leader reads the story – *The Bumblebee Man*.

Getting lost

After this story the assembly leader could use the opportunity to talk about what the children should do if they get lost. (They could invite a policeman to the assembly to talk about this.)

Poem or song

You can choose a poem or a song or both. Select poems and songs which are relevant to the theme or which echo the story in some way.

Examples

Poems:

The Runners (about cooperation)
Page 68 in *Please Mrs Butler* by Allan Ahlberg, published by Puffin, 1984.

Two Lists (going on an errand/not talking to strangers)
Page 94 in *Smile Please* by Tony Bradman, published by Puffin, 1989.

Songs:

One Man's Hands (the power of cooperation)
No. 61 in *Alleluya* (2nd Edition), published by A&C Black, 1980.

Milk Bottle Tops and Paper Bags (cooperation about the environment)
No. 17 in *Someone's Singing Lord* (2nd Edition), published by A&C Black, 2002.

Working Together (cooperation around the world)
No. 37 in *Every Colour Under the Sun*, published by Ward Lock Educational Co. Ltd., 1983.

Quiet reflection or prayer

For a universal, humanistic or multi-faith assembly:

Quiet reflection

The assembly leader says:
"Close your eyes and picture yourself playing or working with a friend. (Pause) There is something very enjoyable about cooperating together. Let us pause to be grateful for opportunities to cooperate with others. (Pause) Let us be happy when we can have a shared project and be helpful and play our part, however small or big our part might be."

Or for Christian schools:

Prayer

Let us pray.

Almighty God,
Thank you for a world in which people cooperate with each other. Help us to fulfil our part when we cooperate with others.

Amen.

Chapter 3

Saving the World
Teacher's Notes

Theme Three: The value of **Empathy**

Values Education: Learning to empathise is part of
Emotional Education

> Very young children are not able to empathise. It is important to
> encourage its development and to recognise its value.

Lesson Plan

This five-part lesson plan is only a guide. Teachers are likely to add to or amend the learning activities which are suggested and may sometimes wish to substitute their own. For any part of the session they may wish to allow more or less time than that suggested.

1 Introduce the theme *5–10 minutes*

What is **empathy**?
The teacher gives examples and explains the value of empathy.
The teacher can link this with understanding and compassion.
The children add some examples of their own and talk about these.

2 Vocabulary *5 minutes*

The teacher ensures that the children understand the words given.
This can be integrated into the reading of the story.

3 The story *5–10 minutes*

The teacher shows the illustration and reads the story.

4 Talking about the story *10–15 minutes*

The teacher uses some of the questions and discussion points given,
stimulating the children to talk about the story/theme.
Some of the questions could be integrated into the reading of the
story.

5 The learning activity *20–35 minutes*

Learning about oxygen/labelling the fish.
Some suggested activities could be used in subsequent, follow-up
lessons.

| Total time | *45–75 minutes* |

1 INTRODUCE THE THEME

Key points

● The concept of 'empathy' is a difficult one for a child.

● Give some examples, such as feeling sorry when your friend hurts herself because you know what the pain feels like, and feeling sad when someone you love is sad.

● Lead the children into giving some examples of their own and talk with the class about these.

● The teacher should explain that when we *feel* sad or happy *with* and *for* another person, we are more likely to be understanding and kind in what we do.

2 VOCABULARY

Use your usual methods for introducing new words.

The difficult words in the story are:

empathy	-	*When we share the emotions of another person; understanding and imaginatively entering their feelings.*
tropical	-	*from the tropics (hot parts of the world)*
patterned	-	*having a recurring design or repeating picture, as on wallpaper*
shimmering	-	*glowing with moving light*
shoal	-	*a group of fish swimming together*
swirled	-	*whirled around*
protect	-	*shield, guard*
fry	-	*baby fish*
leak	-	*drip, escaping water*
anxious	-	*worried*
tepid	-	*slightly warm*
scooped	-	*lifted out with a cup, net or hand*

3 THE STORY:

Saving the World

Amrik imagined how sad his dad would be if all his fish died

Saving the World

Amrik's dad was proud of his tropical fish tank. There, among the waving plants, swam the most beautiful fish he could find. His favourite was a jet-black catfish patterned with spots so bright and round and evenly spaced that to Amrik they looked like yellow polka dots on a blouse. This catfish lived at the bottom of the tank in a tunnel between two stones, rarely coming out, but delighting his dad whenever it did.

Higher in the tank there were lots of guppies with bright tails of shimmering orange silk and a shoal of neon tetras which, like underwater lanterns, glowed with blue light. Often a flying fox swam through the catfish tunnel. The catfish and flying fox were friends.

At the top of the tank lived Amrik's own favourite, a Siamese fighting fish, with magnificent fins, in brilliant red and blue. These swirled about him as he moved. Unfortunately, the Siamese fighting fish was sometimes a bit of a bully, especially to some of the little guppies.

One day, one of these guppies gave birth to lots of baby guppies. Amrik and his dad were thrilled to see such perfect, tiny creatures.

"We'll have to protect them from the big fish," said dad.

From the top of the tank he carefully hung a square net, like a small room, to go under and round the new fry.

"That's a fish nursery to keep them safe," he told Amrik.

"Like a playpen," said Amrik, thinking of his little cousin Rafiq.

"Yes, the tank's like an underwater world," said his dad. "A wonderful world. I think I'd better go and buy some more fish food. Coming Amrik?"

"And some new fish, dad?" Amrik asked.

"Not today son. We need to leave space in the tank for the new guppies to grow. No more new fish from now on I'm afraid."

Amrik was sorry to hear that. He enjoyed going to the water gardens in search of fine fish. But, since this trip was only for fish food, he decided not to go. Instead he switched on the television. A few minutes later, he heard a steady plop, plop sound behind him. He turned to look and saw that water was dripping from one corner of the tank. Suddenly the drip became a steady stream of water, splashing onto the floor.

"Mum!" Amrik shouted, but his mum was in the kitchen on the 'phone to grandma and didn't seem to hear. What could he do? Quickly Amrik emptied the fruit bowl. Apples and oranges rolled across the table. Amrik held the empty bowl under the stream of water. It soon filled up. Amrik poured the water back into the tank and held the bowl under the leak once more. Again and again Amrik held the bowl under the stream of water, emptying it back into the tank as quickly as he could so that he lost as little water as possible onto the floor.

Even so, gradually, the water level fell lower and lower. Amrik almost gave up. His arms were aching and he was bored. It wasn't so much the fish that kept him going, it was the thought of how sad his dad would be if the tank ran dry and all his fish were to die. Amrik imagined his dad coming home with the food for the new fry, his happiness turning to horror when he found an empty tank, all his fish dead on the bottom, even his beautiful cat fish. Sighing, Amrik carried on. Even though he was bored and tired and anxious he continued to cup the leak, while catching the smaller amount of water that still dripped through his fingers.

"Please, please come soon dad," he thought.

As more time passed, the water only just covered the bottom of the baby guppies' net.

"Well the fry will die," Amrik thought, sadly, "but if dad comes in time, I can still save the big fish."

A sudden sound made him jump. His dad had opened the door and was staring across at him.

"Dad!" Amrik shouted with joy.

"Good boy," his dad said, as he took in what was happening. "Can you carry on for a minute?"

Amrik nodded.

"But quick dad. Save the fry quickly."

Dad ran for a drinking glass, filled it with water from the tank and emptied the fry into it, just in time. He then went and found Amrik's mum, who came and took the fruit bowl from Amrik to give him a rest.

Luckily dad had an old tank in the garage. It was smaller than the leaking one but sound. Dad placed this tank by the bigger one. He filled a bowl with tepid water, added some special liquid and filled up the small tank. He transferred the nursery net and poured in the fry. He gave Amrik a small fishing net to catch all the bigger fish. Amrik enjoyed this. He was very careful not to hurt them. One by one he scooped them all out and put them into their new home. Only then was Amrik able to tell his mum and dad what had happened. About hearing the plop of water, about emptying the fruit bowl and about cupping the leak.

"I'm sorry Amrik," his mum said. "I just didn't hear you call."

Amrik told them how bored and tired he had been and how anxious about the level of the water.

"Well you saved the fish, Amrik, even the new babies," said mum. "You did really well. You've saved your dad from a huge disappointment too. He would have been very sad to lose his fish."

"Yes," said his dad. "I certainly would. Thank you Amrik. As a reward, this tank will now be your tank and I will buy another big one and we can find some new fish to go in it."

"Ace," thought Amrik, glad that they would still go on fish hunts. And he was really pleased to have a tank of his own.

"Amrik's tank," his dad said again, "in memory of the day my son saved an underwater world."

4 TALKING ABOUT THE STORY

Did the children understand?

- What did Amrik's dad use to keep the fry safe?

- Where was the tank leaking?

- What did Amrik use to catch the leaking water?

- What else did he do to try to stop the leak?

- What was Amrik's reward?

Points for discussion

- Why do you think Amrik and his dad liked the tropical fish?

- Why did Amrik carry on even when his arms were aching?
  (The opportunity to discuss how empathy helps us to be understanding and kind.)

- Amrik tried not to hurt the fish. Was this empathy too?
  (The opportunity to discuss how we should treat animals even though it is harder for us to understand/ know how they feel.)

5 THE LEARNING ACTIVITY

Links

i)   The activity links with the story through learning more about fish.

ii) The assembly connects with the story through valuing empathy.

iii) If you wish to link the activity to the assembly, display some of the labelled fish. And/or a child can tell/read his or her own adventure story (select one which has the empathy element).

ACTIVITY SUGGESTIONS

- These activities involve working as individuals and as a class.
- The children will need: **1** scissors, glue, rulers and pens.

1 LABELLING FISH

Photocopy the fish page for each child. The children should carefully cut off the word list and then each separate word. They should then glue the fish onto the centre of a sheet of white paper.

Draw the simple fish outline on the black or white board and label each part as shown below. The children should pick out the correct words and stick their labels onto their sheet, adding an arrow pointing to the correct parts of the fish. (This is an opportunity to learn some basic facts about fish and to learn and recognise some associated vocabulary.)

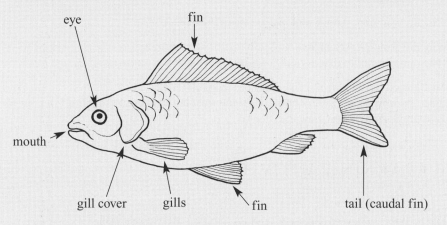

2 UNDERSTANDING FISH

Explain that the fins help the fish to swim in the direction it wants.

Explain that the gills enable the fish to extract oxygen from the water so that it can breath under water. (This is an opportunity to learn about oxygen and breathing – people have lungs to extract oxygen from the air.)

3 CLASS VISIT

If the school has a fish tank, the class can be taken for a 'new' look. It may even be possible to arrange a class outing to visit a tropical fish shop or garden centre with tropical fish, or even a proper aquarium centre.

4 AN ADVENTURE STORY

Amrik had a kind of adventure – saving an underwater world. The children could tell/write an adventure story. It will be a particularly good story if the hero or heroine feels **empathy** for someone they save (as Amrik showed empathy for his dad).

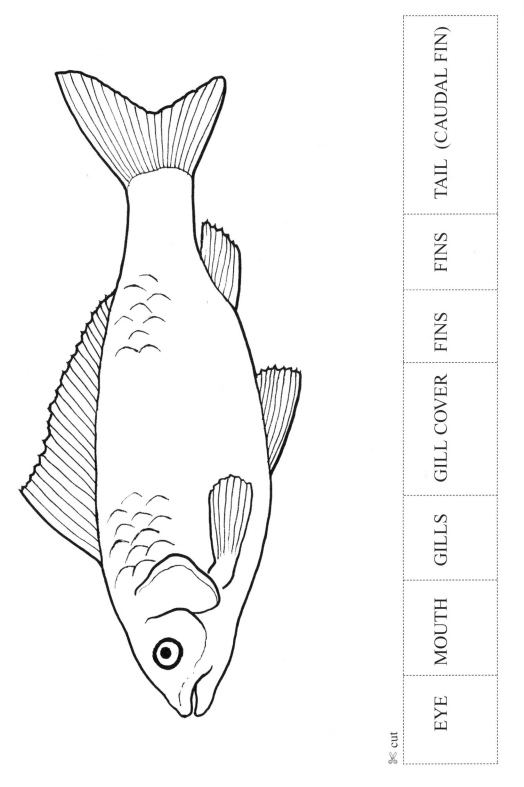

EYE | MOUTH | GILLS | GILL COVER | FINS | FINS | TAIL (CAUDAL FIN)

cut

Assembly

Theme: Empathy

Introduction

The assembly leader introduces the theme and talks about 'empathy'. Empathy is when we feel the emotions of another person. We share how they feel. S/he explains how empathy, therefore, helps us to be more understanding and kind.

Story

Assembly leader:

"Our story today is about a boy, Amrik, who does a great deed. He does a big favour for his dad, because Amrik wants to keep his dad from feeling sad."

The assembly leader reads the story – *Saving the World*.

Poem or song

You can choose a poem or a song or both. Select poems and songs which are relevant to the theme or which echo the story in some way.

A child can read the following poem:

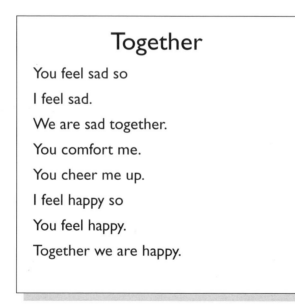

Together

You feel sad so

I feel sad.

We are sad together.

You comfort me.

You cheer me up.

I feel happy so

You feel happy.

Together we are happy.

Other examples

Poems:

Giant Denny (empathy for poor Giant)
Page 33 in *A Second Poetry Book* by John Foster, published by Oxford University Press, 1980.

Autumn (empathy for the birds as winter comes)
Page 84 in *Smile Please* by Tony Bradman, published by Puffin, 1989.

Songs:

Think, Think on These Things (understanding of others)
No. 38 in *Someone's Singing Lord* (2nd Edition), published by A&C Black, 2002.

O Jesus, We are Well and Strong (empathy for the sick and suffering)
No. 4 in *Someone's Singing Lord* (2nd Edition), published by A&C Black, 2002.

Point of View (seeing other people's point of view)
No. 45 in *Every Colour Under the Sun*, published by Ward Lock Educational Co. Ltd., 1983.

Quiet reflection or prayer

For a universal, humanistic or multi-faith assembly:

Quiet reflection

The assembly leader says:
"We feel sad when someone we love is crying. We feel happy when our friend is happy. Let us be glad that we can share in the feelings of other people. (Pause) When someone is sad, let us try to be understanding and kind. When someone is happy, let us try to be happy too. (Pause) A stone does not have life and cannot feel happy or sad. Think about that. Aren't you glad that human beings are alive and have emotions?" (Pause)

Or for Christian schools:

Prayer

Let us pray.

Heavenly Father,
Help us to be sensitive and understanding about the feelings of other people – to try not to hurt their feelings and to be kind when they feel sad. Thank you for creating human beings with emotions – and especially for the wonderful gift of empathy.

Amen.

Chapter 4

The Magician in the Mirror

Teacher's Notes

Theme Four: The value of **Honesty**

Values Education: Learning to be honest is part of **Moral Education**

> In the potentially controversial field of values education, few would dispute the importance of honesty – of teaching children not to steal and not to lie. There are complications even here though, and this story provides an opportunity to distinguish between deceit and make believe and between lies and white lies. It also explores a variety of reasons to be honest.

Lesson Plan

This five-part lesson plan is only a guide. Teachers are likely to add to or amend the learning activities which are suggested and may sometimes wish to substitute their own. For any part of the session they may wish to allow more or less time than that suggested.

1 Introduce the theme   *5–10 minutes*

What is **honesty**?
Include: (a) not stealing and (b) not telling lies. Explain why we should not steal or lie and give examples. (This is another theme which can be linked to 'trust'.) The children add some examples of their own and talk about these.

2 Vocabulary   *5 minutes*

The teacher ensures that the children understand the words given. This can be integrated into the reading of the story.

3 The story   *5–10 minutes*

The teacher shows the illustration and reads the story.

4 Talking about the story   *10–15 minutes*

The teacher uses some of the questions and discussion points given, stimulating the children to talk about the story/theme. Some of the questions could be integrated into the reading of the story.

5 The learning activity   *20–35 minutes*

The children will place cartoon pictures of the story in the correct sequence. An additional potential activity is to use the story of Pinocchio. Some suggested activities could be used in subsequent, follow-up lessons.

Total time | *45–75 minutes*

1 INTRODUCE THE THEME

Key points

● The concept of 'honesty' includes both not stealing and not telling lies.

● You may wish to link these bad behaviours through the concept of 'deceit'.

● You may wish to distinguish between lies (selfish) and white lies (fibs, which we tell in order not to hurt someone's feelings).

● Give examples, such as stealing includes taking something which is not yours and not giving back something which is not yours. Telling lies includes blaming someone for something you did yourself. A white lie would include agreeing that your friend's new coat looks nice when you think it is a horrid colour.

● Lead the children into giving some examples of their own and talk with the class about these.

2 VOCABULARY

Use your usual methods for introducing new words.

The difficult words in the story are:

honesty	-	*being truthful/never to deceive or steal/sincere*
exaggerated	-	*made something seem bigger*
reproach	-	*blame*
comical	-	*amusing, funny*
make-believe	-	*pretend*
fool someone	-	*deceive someone*
rarely	-	*not often*
habit	-	*something you do repeatedly; to act in your usual, established way*
promise	-	*give your word, make a vow*
skilful	-	*do something well*

3 THE STORY:

The Magician in the Mirror

Leo learns to stop telling lies

The Magician in the Mirror

Because he was great fun to play with, Leo had lots of friends. But what none of his friends had found out yet, was that Leo told lies. And on this particular Monday, he told lies one after the other, all day long. It started at breakfast.

"Have you washed your hands, Leo?" his mum asked.

"Yes mum," said Leo, but as he picked up some toast she saw how dirty they were.

"How many times have I told you not to tell lies Leo?" she said. "Go and wash them at once."

Later, on the way to school, Leo said, "I got five gold stars yesterday mum. For good work."

"Well done, darling," his mum said, and then Leo felt bad. It had been only one gold star in fact. His mum would still have been pleased about that. Why had he exaggerated?

"I won't tell any more lies," he thought to himself.

At playtime it was raining so hard that the children had to play inside. Leo and Alan both wanted to play with the Meccano.

"You had it last time," said Leo loudly.

"No, Bruce did," shouted Alan.

Mrs Lester, the playtime lady, heard the quarrel.

"Who had it first?" she asked.

"Me," both boys said, immediately.

Mrs Lester shook her head and took the Meccano away. Alan stared at Leo reproachfully and Leo looked down. They both knew who had really had it first.

After playtime, Miss Garrett the teacher said, "Hands up if you know the story of Pinocchio?"

Leo's hand shot up with several others.

"Good. Well now, Leo, what happened whenever Pinocchio told a lie?"

Leo felt his face go red. How he wished he had kept his hand down.

"It's a wonder your nose isn't huge, Leo," the teacher said. The children laughed.

"You tell us, Megan," said Miss Garrett.

"Every time Pinocchio told a lie, his nose grew bigger," said Megan, giggling.

"What a horrid story," Leo thought, but when Miss Garrett read it to the class, he actually enjoyed it very much.

"Now why shouldn't we tell lies?" Miss Garrett asked, when she had finished reading the story.

"It's not honest," said Joe.

"Yes, good Joe. Now then, what's wrong with that?" said Miss Garrett.

There was a silence.

"What do you think Chloe?" Miss Garrett asked.

"Well, if I stole your bag, Miss Garrett, that wouldn't be honest, and it would make you sad."

"And your tissues are in there," Mat added. He had noticed that Miss Garrett had a cold.

"Yes Chloe," said Miss Garrett. "If you tell a lie it is a bit like stealing – it's stealing the truth. And that's certainly dishonest. And you're right Mat, it does cause problems. If you steal my bag, I haven't got my tissues and if you tell me a lie, about the time of the bus, say, I might miss it."

"My mum says nobody likes a liar," said Megan. "And in the end they always do get found out."

"Yes," said Miss Garrett, "you might not know someone was lying the first time, but if they lie all the time, you always get to know."

Leo thought that Miss Garrett looked at him when she said that.

"Suppose they start to call me 'Leo the liar'," Leo thought. "I would hate that. I really must stop telling any more lies."

But at tea-time, when his mum asked if he had told any lies at school, he immediately said, "No mum," and his hand crept up to his nose to see if it had grown any bigger.

At bedtime, after his mum had tucked him up and said good-night, he thought about Pinocchio again. He touched his nose. Perhaps it did feel as though it was just a little bit bigger. He crept out of bed, switched on the light and stood in front of his mirror to find out. He jumped in fright. Instead of his own reflection, Leo in green pyjamas, there, in the mirror, was a magician in a red cloak, staring back at him.

"Good evening Leo. Don't be frightened. I won't hurt you," said the magician. "In fact, I can't actually climb out of the mirror.

Watch." The magician moved his leg as though to walk through, and the glass of the mirror stopped his foot. It looked so comical that Leo and the magician laughed.

"Who are you?" Leo asked.

"I'm the Mirror-Magician. I'll show you."

He took off his pointed hat and pulled out a rabbit. Next, he showed Leo an empty purse from which he took pound coins one after the other. Best of all, he magiced a glass ball into his empty hands and he and Leo watched the story of Pinocchio swirl inside the glass.

Leo enjoyed all this very much.

"Of course made-up stories like Pinocchio aren't lies," the Mirror-Magician told him. "You see, we know that they are make-believe. They aren't trying to fool anyone. Both the story teller and the story listener know that stories, like tricks for that matter, are all pretend."

"Why have I never seen you before?" Leo asked him.

"I rarely appear to non-mirror children. But listen, Leo, I've come because you're a good boy with a bad habit. I want you to stop telling lies."

Leo felt ashamed.

"I don't mean to," he said. "They just pop out."

"I know," said the Mirror-Magician. "But listen up. If you don't tell a single lie before your next birthday, I'll come on your birthday night and show you some more magic."

Suddenly he was gone, and a small, smiling, blond boy in green pyjamas, Leo's own reflection in fact, was staring back at him.

"Wow," he said, and his reflection, of course, said it too.

Leo desperately wanted to see the Mirror-Magician again.

"I definitely won't tell anymore lies," he thought, and just as he was thinking it, his mum called up to him.

"Leo, are you out of bed?"

"N…" Leo remembered the Mirror-Magician's promise and quickly changed what he had just been about to say. Instead of 'no' he said, "Yes, mum. Sorry. I'm just getting back in."

Of course, the next day, when Leo told his mum about the Mirror-Magician, she didn't believe him. Several times during the next few weeks Leo almost told a lie, but always, just in time, he remembered the Mirror-Magician's promise and told the truth instead.

At long last Leo's birthday arrived. Leo had a great day, but he kept thinking about that night. Would the Mirror-Magician come? Leo hadn't told any lies. Would the Mirror-Magician know that? Surely the Mirror-Magician would keep his promise. After all, to break a promise would be like telling a lie, and the Mirror-Magician hated lies.

By the time Leo went to bed he was bursting with hope that he would see the Mirror-Magician once more. But would he really come?

After his mum had gone downstairs, Leo switched on the light and crossed over to the mirror. In great excitement he looked in and his heart gave a jump with surprise and delight. There, in his red cloak, was the smiling magician.

"Well done Leo," he said.

The Mirror-Magician did some splendid, extra-special magic tricks for Leo's birthday.

After that wonderful night, using his birthday money, Leo bought a box of magic tricks. He practised and practised so that he could become as skilful as the Mirror-Magician, whom he never saw again, though for a long time, whenever he looked in the mirror, Leo hoped that he would be there. After all, it was because of the Mirror-Magician that Leo stopped being 'Leo the Liar' and became the great Magic-Leo instead.

4 TALKING ABOUT THE STORY

Did the children understand?

- How many gold stars did Leo really get?

- Who had really had the Meccano first? Leo or Alan?

- What tricks did the Mirror-Magician show Leo?

- Why didn't Leo's mum believe Leo about seeing the Magician?

- What did Leo do with his birthday money?

Points for discussion

- **Reasons**
  Discuss Chloe's reason for not stealing Miss Garrett's bag. (It would make the teacher sad.) Discuss Miss Garrett's reason for not telling a lie (it's like stealing the truth), Mat's reason (lies cause problems) and Megan's reasons (nobody likes a liar and they always get found out).

- **Lies and make-believe**
  Discuss the difference between lies and make-believe. Try to get the children to understand why we value stories (an enjoyable way of learning without deceit) and why we don't like lies (which are a selfish deceit).

- **Lies and white lies**
  Discuss the difference between lies and white lies.
  (Lies are wrong. White lies, told to save someone's feelings may, some people think, *sometimes* be right.)

- **Promises**
  You could also explore why we should keep our promises.

5 THE LEARNING ACTIVITY

Links

i) The activity links to the story through using this fairly complicated narrative to practise sequencing skills. The material will reinforce the discussions about the value of not telling lies.

ii) The assembly connects with the story through valuing honesty.

iii) If you wish to link the activity to the assembly, children could each read one section of *The Magician in the Mirror* – rehearsing this in advance.

ACTIVITY SUGGESTIONS

- These activities involve working as individuals, as a whole class and as a small group.

- The children will need: **1** 'safe' scissors, glue, paper, rulers and pens **2** video or picture book of Pinocchio.

1 SEQUENCING

Photocopy the cartoon page. The children should draw pictures in the correct sequence.

Help the (older) children with reading the captions.

2 PINOCCHIO

An additional activity would be to tell (or show a video of) the story of Pinocchio.

3 READING PRACTICE

You may also wish to choose five good readers to practise reading a section each of *The Magician in the Mirror*. They could then read the story in the follow-up assembly.

1	2
Leo lied about the Meccano	The magician could not walk out of the mirror
3	**4**
Leo had a great birthday	Leo bought a box of tricks

Assembly

Theme: Honesty and Trust

Introduction

The assembly leader introduces the theme and talks about why we should not steal or tell lies. Link this with trusting people.

Story

Assembly leader:

"Our story today is about how Leo learned not to tell lies. He also learned the difference between lies (deceit), which is bad, and magic tricks (pretend) which is good."

The assembly leader reads the story – *The Magician in the Mirror* (or *Pinocchio*).

And/or:

Five children read *The Magician in the Mirror* – each child reading their own section in sequence.

Child 1 up to: "They both knew who had really had it first."

Child 2 up to: "No mum," and his hand crept up to his nose to see if it had grown any bigger.

Child 3 up to: "I want you to stop telling lies."

Child 4 up to: Several times during the next few weeks Leo almost told a lie, but always, just in time, he remembered the Mirror-Magician's promise and told the truth instead.

Child 5 up to: After all, it was because of the Mirror-Magician that Leo stopped being 'Leo the Liar' and became the great Magic-Leo instead.

Poem or song

You can choose a poem or a song or both. Select poems and songs which are relevant to the theme or which echo the story in some way.

Examples

Poems:

I Did a Bad Thing Once (stealing)
Page 38 in *Please Mrs Butler* by Allan Ahlberg, published by Puffin, 1984.

When We Go Over to My Grandad's (a white lie)
Page 31 in *A First Poetry Book* by Michael Rosen, published by Oxford University Press, 1979.

Songs:

God Bless the Grass (the power of truth)
No. 27 in *Someone's Singing Lord* (2nd Edition), published by A&C Black, 2002.

This train is bound for glory (2nd Edition) (celebration of honest folk)
No. 25 in *Alleluya*, published by A&C Black, 1980.

Quiet reflection or prayer

For a universal, humanistic or multi-faith assembly:

Quiet reflection

The assembly leader says:
"Let us imagine how things would be if everyone told lies all the time. We could trust no one. Promising or making arrangements or giving information or lessons would all be useless. (Pause) Imagine how it would be if everyone stole things all the time. No one would buy anything. No one could keep their favourite things. (Pause) Let us feel grateful for truth and trust. (Pause) Let us resolve not to be liars or thieves or cheats." (Pause).

Or for Christian schools:

Prayer

Let us pray.

Lord God,
We worship you as the God of Truth and we give thanks for all the honest people who do not lie or steal. Give us the strength to be honest and truthful too.

Amen.

Chapter 5

Fireworks for Divali

Teacher's Notes

Theme Five: The value of **Respect for World Religions**

Values Education: Learning to respect the major world religions is part of **Spiritual Education**

> **To know and understand something of world religions is an important part of a good general education. To learn to recognise the fundamental character of spiritual questions and to respect the variety of established responses to these is an important part of spiritual education.**

Lesson Plan

This five-part lesson plan is only a guide. Teachers are likely to add to or amend the learning activities which are suggested and may sometimes wish to substitute their own. For any part of the session they may wish to allow more or less time than that suggested.

1 Introduce the theme   *5–10 minutes*

What is 'Divali' (and Hinduism)?
Give basic information about Hinduism and about Divali.
Mention some of the major celebrations of other world religions.

2 Vocabulary   *5 minutes*

The teacher ensures that the children understand the words given. This can be integrated into the reading of the story.

3 The story   *5–10 minutes*

The teacher shows the illustration and reads the story.

4 Talking about the story   *10–15 minutes*

The teacher uses some of the questions and discussion points given, stimulating the children to talk about the story/theme.
Some of the questions could be integrated into the reading of the story.

5 The learning activity   *20–35 minutes*

The children will each make a Divali card.
Some suggested activities could be used in subsequent, follow-up lessons.

| **Total time** | *45–75 minutes* |

1 INTRODUCE THE THEME

Key points

● Using a large map, show the children where India is. (In a multicultural school the teacher can ask: Do you know anyone who came to live here from India? Your parents or grandparents?) The teacher points out how big and diverse India is – with many languages: Punjabi, Gujerati, etc. and many religions: Hinduism, Sikhism, Islam, Buddhism, Christianity. Tell the children about Divali. (The story is about Jasmine, a Hindu girl, who didn't want to miss the Divali fireworks.)

● This is an opportunity for children to learn that all the major religions have celebrations. Explain that celebrations bring people together, reminding everyone about important events. What other religious celebrations are there, in Christianity for example. What does your family do to celebrate Christmas? Or Divali? Or Eide? Discuss similarities and differences between these celebrations.

● For further information you could consult:
Hinduism by Sue Penny, published by Heinemann Educational Books, 2000
Introduction to World Religions, published by Dorling Kindersley.

2 VOCABULARY

Use your usual methods for introducing new words.

The difficult words in the story are:

Divali	-	*Hindu festival of lights*
the temple	-	*(Hindu) place of worship*
feverish	-	*hot with an illness*
suffused	-	*softly covered; spread through*
magic	-	*supernatural power*
banquet	-	*great feast*
celebrations	-	*ritualistic community events/parties; special festivities*
magnificent	-	*splendid*
recognised	-	*found something or someone familiar – known before*

3 THE STORY:

Fireworks for Divali

Jasmine has her own Divali celebration

Fireworks for Divali

It was the night before Divali and Jasmine always loved the temple fireworks, but this year, feverish and sore with chicken pox, she knew that she would have to stay at home. She felt very sad about this. Even so, tossing and turning in her tangled sheets, trying hard not to scratch the itchy red spots, she longed for the morning to come.

"Don't be sad," whispered a shadow-soft voice.

Jasmine sat up. She could hardly believe her eyes. At the end of her bed, suffused by a gentle glow, was the most beautiful fairy you could ever imagine. Everything about her was a shimmering gold – her gleaming gold sari, her feathery yellow wings and her amber brown eyes. Even her long, straight hair, glossy as conkers, glinted with buttercups brighter than beads. Reaching out, she smiled at Jasmine, who somehow found herself hand in hand with the fairy, and dressed not in her nightdress but in her favourite turquoise sari.

"Don't be afraid," said the golden fairy. Slowly they rose from the bed and flew gently toward the open window, and out into the night sky. The air felt cool on Jasmine's hot cheeks.

With arms outstretched, still holding the fairy's hand, she glided effortlessly above the tallest trees. Below, she could see the scattered lights of houses and the moving lights of cars. It was wonderful to fly but after a time they began to descend. They landed, gently, in the courtyard of a palace. There Jasmine was amazed and delighted to see magical creatures from every story ever told – elves, wizards, and even a white unicorn with a golden horn. A long table offered a banquet of magical dishes.

To Jasmine's surprise a tree moved forward slightly and actually spoke to her in a deep, woody voice.

"Help yourself my dear," said the tree.

Jasmine ate some delicious, blue ice-cream which soothed her sore throat.

"Now for the fireworks," said the golden fairy.

It was the best firework display Jasmine had ever been to. It began, like other firework shows, with showers of coloured lights, green and red and silver against the dark sky.

The Story

"Ooh" and "Ahh" everyone said, as the cascades of light burst and blossomed above their heads. But the finale was more wonderful than any ordinary firework display could be. The fireworks formed a moving image, like a huge movie screen, across the darkness. Clearly, and with great beauty, the firework pictures told the story of Rama and Sita. First everyone saw Prince Rama sent away by his father. They watched Rama and his beautiful wife Sita living in a forest of green firework trees. Next Ravana, the demon king, captured Sita. The watchers saw Rama and his army rescue her and return to their own kingdom. As the final fireworks pictured Rama being crowned and showed the welcoming crowds full of joy, in the courtyard the real crowd of story book watchers gave a mighty cheer.

Afterwards, Jasmine could never remember the journey home. She couldn't even remember saying goodbye to the fairy, though she hoped she had said thank you. No, the next thing Jasmine remembered was being wakened by her mother bringing in a breakfast tray.

"You look much better," she said, feeling Jasmine's forehead.

"Good. Your temperature's down. But, my dear, I'm afraid you're still not well enough for the Divali celebrations. I know you're disappoi..."

"No! Listen mum ..." With great excitement, Jasmine told her night adventure.

"What an exciting dream you've had," her mother said. "And look, here's a Divali present."

"Thanks mum," Jasmine said, as she took the silver parcel. She untied the scarlet ribbon. Somehow she no longer minded about missing the celebrations. After all, dream or not, she had been to a magnificent firework display already.

Inside the parcel was a book full of poems about flower fairies, with lovely pictures. And, later, as Jasmine read her new book, on the very last page she found a picture which she recognised. Jasmine smiled thoughtfully. It was a picture of a golden fairy, with sunny buttercups threaded through her hair.

4 TALKING ABOUT THE STORY

Did the children understand?

- Why was Jasmine sad at first?

- What did the golden fairy look like?

- What did Jasmine eat at the banquet?

- Why was Jasmine not disappointed in the end?

- What was her Divali gift?

Points for discussion

- **The difference between magic and religion**
  What is the difference between a dream and reality?
  What is the difference between magic and science?
  (Magic – make-believe, science – true/real, etc.)
  What is the difference between magical make-believe (e.g. fairies) and religious figures from the past (e.g. Rama and Sita)?
  (Fairies – pretend, religious figures – real and revered, etc.)
  What is the difference between magic and religion?
  (Magic – superstition or pretend, religion – rational faith, etc.)

- **Hinduism**
  Do the children know the story of Rama and Sita?
  Do the children understand Divali?
  Do the children understand that there are several world faiths?

- **Respecting other faiths**
  Why should we respect religious beliefs that are different from our own? (Talk about how religions try to answer the most fundamental/important questions: about the meaning of life, about creation and the creator, about why we are here and how we should live. Therefore, a person's religion is of central importance for who they are.)

5 THE LEARNING ACTIVITY

Links

i)   The activity links with the story through a focus on Divali.

ii) The assembly connects with the story through valuing all major world religions.

iii) If you wish to link the activity to the assembly, the children's Divali cards can be displayed.

ACTIVITY SUGGESTIONS

- These activities involve working as individuals.
- The children will need coloured pencils.

I MAKING A DIVALI CARD

Photocopy the activity page. The children can colour the 'Happy Divali' message and write in their name. They then fold along the dotted line to produce a card. They should do their own picture of a candle, or of fireworks, on the front cover.

(The cards could be sent, with a letter from the children, for Divali, to a Hindu temple, or displayed, at Divali, on the classroom walls.)

2 WRITING A CELEBRATION POEM

In addition the children could write a poem about a family *celebration* (about Christmas or Divali, etc.). Some of these could be rehearsed for reading in the assembly. (Younger children could draw a celebration picture.)

3 CLASSROOM

You could write a joint class poem. Take the words 'celebration is ...' and encourage the children to begin each line of the poem with 'Celebration is ...'. Several children could each read a verse in the assembly.

Happy Divali

Assembly

Theme: **Respect for World Religions**

Introduction

The assembly leader introduces the theme and talks about the importance, to people, of their religious beliefs. These are beliefs about the fundamental things: creation and the creator; the purpose of human life (why we are here); the meaning of our own life and about how we should live. This is why we should show respect for all the world religions: Christianity, Islam, Hinduism, Judaism, Sikhism, Buddhism and so on.

Story

Assembly leader:

"Our story today is about a Hindu girl who did not want to miss the Divali celebrations."

The assembly leader reads the story – *Fireworks for Divali*.

And/or:

The assembly leader or a child reads the story of Rama and Sita.

Poem or song

You can choose a poem or a song or both, or some of the children could read their celebration poem and/or the joint class poem 'Celebration is'. Select poems and songs which are relevant to the theme or which echo the story in some way.

Examples

Poems:

Why? (fundamental questions)
Page 123 in *A Second Poetry Book* by Phoebe Hesketh, published by Oxford University Press, 1980.

The Cliff-Top (the beauty of heaven and earth)
Page 46 in *A First Poetry Book* by Robert Bridges and Jane Catermull, published by Oxford University Press, 1979.

Who? (the mystery of creation)
Page 123 in *A First Poetry Book* by Robert Bridges and Jane Catermull, published by Oxford University Press, 1979.

Songs:

When I Needed a Neighbour (people of all faiths are my neighbour)
No. 35 in *Someone's Singing Lord* (2nd Edition), published by A&C Black, 2002.

The Ink is Black, the Page is White (the beauty of respect for all groups)
No. 39 in *Someone's Singing Lord* (2nd Edition), published by A&C Black, 2002.

I Believe (an expression of faith)
No. 20 in *Every Colour Under the Sun*, published by Ward Lock Educational Co. Ltd., 1983

Quiet reflection or prayer

For a universal, humanistic or multi-faith assembly:

Quiet reflection

The assembly leader says:
"Let us all think quietly to ourselves about what we believe. (Pause) Let us also respect the different religious beliefs of others. (Pause) We recognise the great importance of the questions which religions try to answer: about creation, about how we should live and why we are here. Let us think about these questions. (Pause)

Or for Christian schools:

Prayer

Let us pray.

Almighty God,
We pray to you, the Creator of Everything, who is worshipped all over the world in many different ways. Remind us to think about the great questions and show each of us how to live a good life – how to relate to other people, to your world, and to you.
Amen.

Chapter 6

Free as the Wind

Teacher's Notes

Theme Six: The value of **Independence** and **Determination**

Values Education: Developing a spirit of independence and determination is part of **Personal Education**

> **We continuously help children to develop their skills and thus to become more independent. It is important to recognise the child's own will to independence, but also the uneven path for some and often their determination and courage in the face of difficulties. It is important, too, not to lose sight of the value of interdependence. Children need to learn how to help others without patronisation and how to recognise when they, too, need help. We all need to receive help graciously and without loss of self-esteem.**

Lesson Plan

This five-part lesson plan is only a guide. Teachers are likely to add to or amend the learning activities which are suggested and may sometimes wish to substitute their own. For any part of the session they may wish to allow more or less time than that suggested.

1 Introduce the theme   *5–10 minutes*

What is **independence**?
How being independent gives us greater self-esteem and more freedom.
How, sometimes, we need to be **determined**, to persevere, in order to gain a new skill.

2 Vocabulary   *5 minutes*

The teacher ensures that the children understand the words given.
This can be integrated into the reading of the story.

3 The story   *5–10 minutes*

The teacher shows the illustration and reads the story.

4 Talking about the story   *10–15 minutes*

The teacher uses some of the questions and discussion points given, stimulating the children to talk about the story/theme.
Some of the questions could be integrated into the reading of the story.

5 The learning activity   *20–35 minutes*

The children will colour in the story illustration and add details of their own. Some suggested activities could be used in subsequent, follow-up lessons.

Total time | *45–75 minutes*

1 INTRODUCE THE THEME

Key points

● Children readily understand the satisfaction of doing things for themselves. Ask them for examples of things they have already learned to do.

● Children also understand that learning how to do something can be difficult and needs practice. Ask for examples of new skills the children want to develop.

● But children also need to understand that we all need to depend on each other too – and be helpful.

● Children need to understand that some things are harder for some people. People should not be blamed for failing. The important thing is to try. Determination is a kind of courage.

2 VOCABULARY

Use your usual methods for introducing new words.

The difficult words in the story are:

independence	-	*ability to do something without help or interference; not reliant on another*
frustrating	-	*preventing you from doing something, making you tense, anxious, unsatisfied and upset*
coordination	-	*(hands and eyes) working well together*
embarrassment	-	*feeling ashamed or self-conscious*
manage	-	*do something, though with some difficulty*
mount	-	*climb onto a horse*
intently	-	*strongly and purposefully*
sympathy	-	*kindly understanding; sharing another's sorrow; pity*

3 THE STORY:

Free as the Wind

Jane was determined to mount Dobbin by herself

Free as the Wind

When Jane came home from the hospital, she found that there were things which she had been able to do before her illness, such as catching a ball, which she now had to learn to do all over again. It was very frustrating. One day she decided to draw a picture of her dog, Inky, and the lines she drew came out kind of shaky. Disappointed with herself, she scribbled all over the picture.

"Don't be upset, Jane," her mummy said. "Your illness has left you with a coordination problem. It makes things more difficult, but you'll manage in the end. You'll see." And slowly, Jane's drawings improved.

After a few months, Jane went back to her nursery school. She was really pleased to see her friend Anna again. They smiled at each other, but when Anna unbuttoned her coat and hung it onto her peg, to Jane's embarrassment, Jane needed the teacher's help to do the same thing.

Later in the day, Jane felt even worse. In one corner of the nursery there was a large, wooden rocking-horse called Dobbin. Jane had always loved climbing onto Dobbin and riding him. But seeing how big he was, she knew that she just might not manage to climb on and she didn't want Mrs Fox to come and help her. She felt very sad. That night, at home, as she stroked Inky's silky, black fur, she talked to her little dog about it.

"I wish I was like I used to be," she said, and Inky cocked his head to one side, listening intently. "Most of all, I wish I could still ride Dobbin." Inky wagged his tail in sympathy.

The next day, back at nursery school, Jane noticed that the teacher, Mrs Fox, was busy talking to Anna's mum. Jane seized the chance to try to climb on Dobbin without help. She put one foot in the strap and pulled on the reins, trying very hard to climb over like she used to do. Somehow, she slipped back down. She tried again. And again. And again. Each time she fell back down she wanted to scream or cry. Suddenly, she noticed that Mrs Fox was hurrying over to help her. "I will do it by myself," thought Jane, and making a huge effort, she flung her body upwards, pulling tight on the reins, and somehow she just about managed to mount the big horse. There she was, as high as a king.

"Well done Jane," said Mrs Fox.

"I won't fall Miss," said Jane. "I'll be all right by myself."

Mrs Fox hesitated. Then she smiled.

"Well hold on one minute Jane. Don't ride him just for a minute."

The teacher went and fetched a thick rubber mat and placed it by Dobbin. The other teacher, Miss Moor, arrived with another mat, which she placed on the other side of the horse. Both teachers then went away.

Jane rode and rode, faster and faster, for ages and ages, a beaming smile on her face. In her imagination, Dobbin became a real horse. The nursery and the playing children faded away and she was galloping over the fields, free as the wind, once again riding Dobbin, all by herself.

4 TALKING ABOUT THE STORY

Did the children understand?

- Why did Jane have to learn some things over again?

- Why did Jane scribble on her picture of Inky?

- Why did Jane have a coordination problem?

- What wishes did Jane tell Inky?

- Why did the teachers put mats by Dobbin?

Points for discussion

- **Trying is important**
  Discuss why Jane found things difficult and why she felt embarrassed.
  Discuss how brave and determined Jane was.
  Ask the children what they find difficult.

- **Interdependence**
  Discuss why it is good to be independent (freedom, self-esteem) but also why it is
  good to be interdependent (ready to give and to receive help when necessary).

5 THE LEARNING ACTIVITY

Links

i)   The activity links with the story through the image of Jane (riding, free as the wind,
     because she is free to mount Dobbin by herself). It also allows the children to imag-
     ine the meadow for themselves – as Jane did.

ii) The assembly connects with the story through valuing independence and determina-
     tion – but within a humane interdependence.

iii) If you wish to link the activity to the assembly, the children's pictures can be dis-
     played and/or the children can *practise* a new song to be used in the assembly.

ACTIVITY SUGGESTIONS

● These activities involve working as individuals and as a class.
● The children will need coloured pencils.

1 THE PICTURE

Photocopy the picture for the children. This has been drawn to allow them to carefully colour-in Jane on the horse (coordination) and to use their own imagination by adding elements to the meadow – perhaps flowers, birds, a tree, clouds in the sky, etc.

2 PRACTISE A SKILL

This is an opportunity to practise a skill which the children are *currently* in the process of acquiring – taking on Jane's determination!

3 A NEW SONG

You could also take the opportunity to introduce a new, rather difficult song which the class will need to practise. This could then be sung at the assembly.

Assembly

Theme: Independence, Determination and Interdependence

Introduction

The assembly leader introduces the theme of independence. How and why we like to be independent. How learning helps us to be independent. How determination helps us to master new skills because we have to practise and persevere. Nevertheless, how we all need other people and should be helpful to each other. Interdependence is valuable too.

Story

Assembly leader:

"Our story today is about Jane, a brave young girl whose determination helped her to become more independent. Jane's imagination, as well as her independence, allowed her to be 'free as the wind'."

The assembly leader reads the story – *Free as the Wind*.

Poem or song

You can choose a poem or a song or both. Alternatively, the class could sing a new song which they have practised for the assembly. Select poems and songs which are relevant to the theme or which echo the story in some way.

Examples

Poems:

All on My Own (being independent and dependent)
Page 26 in *Smile Please* by Tony Bradman, published by Puffin, 1989.

Scarecrow Independence (be proud of who we are)
Page 102 in *A First Poetry Book* by James Kirkup, published by Oxford University Press, 1979.

Songs:

For All the Strength we Have (praise for strength, skills and health)
No. 6 in *Someone's Singing Lord* (2nd Edition), published by A&C Black.

Don't You Think We're Lucky? (happy that we can do things)
No. 25 in *Every Colour Under the Sun* published by Ward Lock Educational Co. Ltd., 1983.

Quiet reflection or prayer

For a universal, humanistic or multi-faith assembly:

Quiet reflection

The assembly leader says:
"Close your eyes and picture Jane riding through the meadow. (Pause) Let us be under-standing of the needs of those who have been ill. Let us be helpful to them. (Pause) Let us value Jane's determination and be determined in what we attempt ourselves. (Pause) Let us value independence and yet also value, as human beings, our interdependence – our sup-port of each other. (Pause)

Or for Christian schools:

Prayer

Let us pray.

Lord God,
Thank you for our ability to learn new skills. Help us to try hard. Help us too, dear God, to be helpful to others and to have the grace to receive help. We pray that you will give strength and peace to those who are sick or are recovering from sickness.

Amen.

Chapter 7

Finding Dragon Land

Teacher's Notes

Theme Seven: The value of **Sharing**

Values Education: Learning to share is part of **Social Education**

> Learning to share does not always come easily! Nevertheless, it is often a practical, and for children an understandable, form of being fair. Thus sharing, as well as being important for good social relations, is an important element in moral development too.

Lesson Plan

This five-part lesson plan is only a guide. Teachers are likely to add to or amend the learning activities which are suggested and may sometimes wish to substitute their own. For any part of the session they may wish to allow more or less time than that suggested.

1 Introduce the theme   *5–10 minutes*

What is **sharing**?
Talk about sharing toys and sweets. The children understand about this.
The children add some examples of their own and talk about these.

2 Vocabulary   *5 minutes*

The teacher ensures that the children understand the words given.
This can be integrated into the reading of the story.

3 The story   *5–10 minutes*

The teacher shows the illustration and reads the story.

4 Talking about the story   *10–15 minutes*

The teacher uses some of the questions and discussion points given, stimulating the children to talk about the story/theme.
Some of the questions could be integrated into the reading of the story.

5 The learning activity   *20–35 minutes*

An opportunity to focus on the hissing sound of letter 'S' and the soft, shushing sound of 'sh'. The children illustrate the story.
Some suggested activities could be used in subsequent, follow-up lessons.

Total time | *45–75 minutes*

INTRODUCE THE THEME

Key points

- The concept of 'sharing' is a familiar one for most children. You could stretch their understanding by including learning to share non-material things such as 'attention' (e.g. with a new baby in the family).

- You could contrast 'sharing' with being selfish. Give examples and encourage the children to give examples of their own.

- Sharing can be linked to being friendly and making friends. (How do we feel when someone shares their toys/games with us?)

- Sam shows various valuable moral qualities – helpfulness, kindness, courage. Sharing tends to encourage such attributes.

VOCABULARY

Use your usual methods for introducing new words.

The difficult words in the story are:

sharing	-	*giving part (often half) of something to another person*
unwilling	-	*reluctant, doing something you don't really want to do*
spiky	-	*pointed and sharp, like a thorn or needle*
woodland creature	-	*animal that lives in woods*
munched	-	*chewed up/crunched*
splendid	-	*wonderful*
delicious	-	*tasty/scrumptious*

3 THE STORY:

Finding Dragon Land

Sam shares his lunch with Dyfed

Finding Dragon Land

Sam was walking unwillingly to school. He was dreading the Monday morning spelling test. "I can't miss it though," he thought. He knew that if you were late for school, his teacher could be as fierce as a dragon.

"Help," he heard someone shout. "Help."

Sam could hardly believe his eyes. There in front of him was a real dragon – a baby dragon with one of its wings caught in a spiky bush.

"Please boy, will you help me?" it pleaded, tearfully.

Now because dragons can breathe fire Sam was a bit scared. But he was sorry for the small creature, and putting down his bag for a moment, he helped it to get free.

"Thanks," said the dragon. "I'm Dyfed by the way."

"I'm Sam. I've never met a dragon before."

"We don't often leave Dragon Land." The dragon looked worried. "As a matter of fact, I'm lost. Will you help me to get home?"

"I could take you to my teacher. She would help," Sam offered.

"Dragons never go to school," Dyfed said, firmly. "To reach Dragon Land we have to find a special magic word beginning with 'S' and whisper it to a woodland creature."

"What word?" asked Sam.

"If I could remember, I wouldn't be lost, would I?" said Dyfed. "I've completely forgotten. I'm not very good at spelling."

Sam didn't want to think about spelling.

"Nor me neither," he said. "So, what can we do?"

"Come on. Let's go into the woods to play. That's where the woodland creatures are and I might remember the magic word."

In the woods they saw birds and squirrels.

"'Squirrel' begins with 'S', I think," said Sam. "Well it's not squirrel," said Dyfed.

Sam and Dyfed found a stream which splashed over stones like a small waterfall. They sailed sticks over it.

"Is the word 'stream'?" said Sam. "That begins with an 'S'."

"No," said Dyfed.

"Or 'stick' or 'stone'?" said Sam.

Dyfed shook his head, sadly.

Sam had an idea.

"My name begins with an 'S'," he said, "and my mum says I'm special."

"Well it's not Sam," said Dyfed.

He was beginning to get worried, and since it was nearly lunchtime, he was beginning to get hungry too.

"I'm hungry," said Dyfed.

Sam took the lunch box out of his bag and they sat down on a flat stone near the stream. Sam was also very hungry and he only had lunch for one person, but he couldn't leave his new friend without any food. Carefully and kindly he shared his sandwiches – two for Sam and two for Dyfed. He divided his orange and his orange juice in half and broke his Kit-Kat into two fingers – one each.

The two friends munched in silence, hungrily.

"Could the word be 'sandwich'?" asked Sam.

As Dyfed shook his head, two fat tears rolled down his baby dragon face. He felt very lost indeed.

"However will I get home?" he asked.

"Don't cry Dyfed," said Sam, wondering what on earth they could do.

"You've been very kind Sam," Dyfed gulped, "and th-thank you for sharing your lunch with me."

Suddenly his face lit up. "Sharing your lunch," he repeated. He sprang to his feet and flapped his little dragon wings in excitement. A lick of flame came from his mouth.

"Careful," said Sam, moving back.

"Sharing!" shouted Dyfed. "Sharing is a splendid, special thing in Dragon Land. That's our magic word!"

"Does 'sharing' begin with 'S'?" asked Sam, doubtfully.

Dyfed nodded, grinning from ear to ear. He pointed to a butterfly on a bush nearby. Sam and Dyfed leaned towards it and whispered, 'sharing.'

They laughed in delight as they were whirled through the clouds to Dragon Land.

The dragons were pleased to see Dyfed the Small. They thanked Sam for helping and gave him a toy dragon. They also gave Sam and Dyfed a second lunch – the special ABC Dragon-

Land lunch. Apricots and Bananas with Chocolate Sauce. It was delicious.

"Now climb on my back, Sam, and hold tight," said Dyfed's dad.

The big, green dragon flew all the way back to Sam's school. For Sam it was a wonderful ride instead of a horrid spelling test, and his teacher was so surprised to see him arrive on a dragon, she forgot that he was late.

4 TALKING ABOUT THE STORY

Did the children understand?

- Why was Sam unwilling to go to school?
- How did Dyfed need help?
- What was the magic word?
- What was the special ABC Dragon Land lunch?
- What made Sam's teacher forget that he was late?

Points for discussion

- Are dragons real? What is the difference between real and imaginary?
- Sam was scared but nevertheless helped Dyfed. To be *brave* is to do something when you are afraid.
- Why is sharing a good thing to do?
  (Friendship bonds; kindness; being fair.)
- There are dragons in many stories. Do the children also know about the Welsh Dragon (who looks like Dyfed, of course) and about the Chinese (New Year) Dragon, and the story of St George and the Dragon?

5 THE LEARNING ACTIVITY

Links

i)   The activity links to the story through the letter 'S' and through doing an 'illustration'.

ii) The assembly connects with the story through valuing sharing (and related valuable qualities).

iii) If you wish to link the activity to the assembly you can display the children's illustration of the story and/or use one of their own stories about sharing.

ACTIVITY SUGGESTIONS

- These activities involve working as individuals but with the sharing of crayons/pencils.

- The children will need several complete sets of coloured pencils or crayons – one set per pair of children or one set to be shared between one table group.

I 'S' AND 'SH'

Explain that the letter 'S' (use its name) can make the 'S' sound as in 'sun' or 'squirrel', but it can also make the 'sh' sound when combined with the letter 'h' (two letters making one sound is called a *digraph*).

Photocopy the template. Ask the children to brainstorm words beginning with the letter 'S' and write them inside the large outline of the 'S'. If time allows, the children could draw pictures to go with some of the words around the outside of the page.

Older children could, in a follow-up session, draw a large, open 'sh' and do a similar exercise for 'sh'.

2 ILLUSTRATION

Allow each child to do an illustration which matches the story. (They can choose whatever part they want, e.g. Sam untangling Dyfed from the spiky bush or sharing his lunch with Dyfed, or Sam riding on the big dragon.) Allow only one set of coloured pencils between two children (they must share these as they work).

3 WRITING A STORY

Older children could write and illustrate their own story about sharing. One of these could be selected for reading in the assembly.

SUN

Assembly

Theme: Sharing

Introduction

The assembly leader introduces the theme and talks about sharing, and why it is a good thing to do.

Story

Assembly leader:

"Our story today is about a brave and kind boy, Sam, who knew how to share."

The assembly leader reads the story – *Finding Dragon Land*.

And/or:

One or more of the children could read their own story about sharing.

Poem or song

You can choose a poem or a song or both. Select poems and songs which are relevant to the theme or which echo the story in some way.

Examples

Poems:

August Afternoon (about sharing a lemonade)
Page 79 in *A First Poetry Book* by Marion Edey, published by Oxford University Press, 1979.

The Sick Young Dragon (about a young dragon)
Page 74 in *A Very First Poetry Book* by John Foster, published by Oxford University Press, 1984.

Songs:

Hands to Work and Feet to Run (sharing God's good gifts)
No. 21 in *Someone's Singing Lord* (2nd Edition), published by A&C Black, 2002.

Stick on a Smile (sharing, helping and smiling for a happy world)
No. 43 in *Every Colour Under the Sun*, published by Ward Lock Educational Co. Ltd., 1983.

Quiet reflection or prayer

For a universal, humanistic or multi-faith assembly:

Quiet reflection

The assembly leader says:
"Wasn't Sam a great kid? Wouldn't he be a good friend? Think about how he was compassionate, brave and kind and about how he shared his lunch, even though he was hungry. (Pause) Let us learn how to share like Sam. Think now of some ways you could share with your family and friends." (Pause)

Or for Christian schools:

Prayer

Let us pray.

Almighty God,
Help us to be compassionate and kind and to be willing to share.
Amen.

Chapter 8

A Pattern of Pleasure

Teacher's Notes

Theme Eight: The value of **Creativity**

Values Education: Learning to be creative is part of our
Emotional Education

> There are two aspects to the development of creativity. First,
> children should experience the satisfaction of self-expression. They
> express their own choices and personality in what they make. But,
> secondly, children need to understand standards of excellence in
> the various fields of creativity so that they can strive toward these
> – to make their creations as worthwhile as possible.

Lesson Plan

This five-part lesson plan is only a guide. Teachers are likely to add to or amend the learning activities which are suggested and may sometimes wish to substitute their own. For any part of the session they may wish to allow more or less time than that suggested.

1 Introduce the theme *5–10 minutes*

What is **creativity**?
The teacher explains that we can be creative in many different fields
and forms – giving examples. The children add some examples of
their own and talk about these.

2 Vocabulary *5 minutes*

The teacher ensures that the children understand the words given. This
can be integrated into the reading of the story.

3 The story *5–10 minutes*

The teacher shows the illustration and reads the story.

4 Talking about the story *10–15 minutes*

The teacher uses some of the questions and discussion points given,
stimulating the children to talk about the story/theme. Some of the
questions could be integrated into the reading of the story.

5 The learning activity *20–35 minutes*

Creating their own autumn leaf collage.
Some suggested activities could be used in subsequent,
follow-up lessons.

Total time | *45–75 minutes*

1 INTRODUCE THE THEME

Key points

- Children already understand the pleasure of making things. The idea of making something as well as they possibly can, using their own imagination and their own choices (e.g. of colours) will, therefore, not be too difficult to understand.

- Give examples to show the many fields in which people can be creative. Include the arts: painting, sculpture, writing stories and poems; the crafts: sewing, making jewellery, etc.; the sciences: inventing new objects, discovering new ways of understanding the universe. But also include day-to-day ways in which people express themselves: e.g. planting a garden, choosing stylish clothes, etc. Can the children give examples?

- Give and receive examples of ways in which we can try to be more creative: with colour and shapes in our paintings (combining them in new and pleasing ways) and with language in our poems and stories (choosing interesting and vivid words and phrases), etc.

- There are two aspects to being creative:
  (a) We *express ourselves* – that is, we make something unique because no one else would make exactly the same thing. We make our own choices of colour etc.
  (b) We make something *worthwhile* – that is, we make something as well as we can, something that others will find pleasing and stimulating too. It *communicates* (new) ideas or emotions to others.

2 VOCABULARY

Use your usual methods for introducing new words.

The difficult words in the story are:

creativity	-	*the gift of making something new*
twirling	-	*twisting in the air*
fluttering	-	*soft beating, like wings*
random	-	*by chance*
pattern	-	*a design*
random pattern	-	*a design made by chance*
felt	-	*a thick, slightly hairy fabric*
autumn	-	*third season of the year – between summer and winter (September-December)*
efforts	-	*tries/attempts*
favourite	-	*most liked*
ruined	-	*spoiled*
overlapping	-	*partly covering*
curvy	-	*having a rounded shape*
full to the brim	-	*full to the top*
scented	-	*perfumed*

3 THE STORY:

A Pattern of Pleasure

Azra experienced the pleasure of making a beautiful thing

A Pattern of Pleasure

Side by side at the window, Azra and her mum watched as golden leaves drifted down from the trees, twirling and fluttering like flocks of yellow butterflies. Their brightness made a random pattern on the red and orange leaves already down.

"Aren't the autumn colours wonderful!" said Azra's mum. "But come on darling, I want to take this bag of clothes to the Oxfam shop. Just check first for your dressing up."

Azra kept old clothes in a box in her bedroom. She enjoyed playing dressing-up games with her friend.

"That long black scarf would be good," she said, because sometimes she dressed up as the old woman who lived in a shoe, pretending that her dolls were the children. "And these to use for dolls' blankets," she added, collecting several squares of felt which were left over from when her mum had made soft toy dogs for the school bring and buy. Azra's mum folded the scarf and added it to Azra's pile of felt squares.

"I must get a new scarf to go with my new black coat," she said. "Now, pop those up to your room, Azra, and we'll be off."

As Azra walked to the shops with her mum, she fingered a silver fifty-pence piece in her pocket. Her mum's birthday was the following week, and Azra had saved the fifty pence to buy a present. Although her dad always bought something for Azra to give to mum, this year Azra wanted to surprise them both by giving a present of her very own choice.

In the Oxfam shop, while mum was talking to the shop lady, Azra had a quick look round. Because mum loved the autumn colours, and had an autumn birthday, Azra wanted to find a present in red or orange or yellow. She saw a purse covered with bright red beads, but that cost five pounds, much more than she had. She spotted some earrings shaped like golden leaves, but they were also too expensive. Soon it was time to walk home again, and Azra still hadn't found the right gift.

"Never mind," she thought to herself, "I've got a whole week left. If I tell Grandma in secret, she'll bring me to look round the shops."

At home, as Azra took off her coat, she felt again in the pocket. What a shock! To her dismay, the fifty pence had gone. Somehow it had fallen out and got lost. Although Azra felt very upset, she said nothing to her mum. Instead, that evening when Grandma came to look after her, Azra told Grandma what had happened. Grandma immediately offered to give Azra another fifty pence, but somehow that didn't help.

"You see Grandma," Azra tried to explain, "I want to do this present all by myself. I saved the fifty pence in secret. If you just give me another, it's like daddy just buying the present for me. You see?"

"I understand," said Grandma. "You want your present to be by your own efforts and your own choice." She thought for a moment.

"You know, Azra, the best presents are those people make for us with love and care. Why don't you do an autumn painting?"

"Because I've already done an autumn picture on the birthday card I've made."

Azra knew she sounded cross. She felt quite sulky and as though it was all Grandma's fault, which of course it wasn't.

Grandma cheered Azra up by telling her some of their favourite stories about the olden days, but that night, when Azra lay in bed, all her disappointment returned. She imagined how surprised her mum and dad would have been by her extra, secret present, and now she couldn't buy one. "My plan is ruined," she thought, as she finally fell asleep, but, when Azra woke up the next morning, she woke up with a wonderful idea.

That day she collected some leaves from the garden, choosing flat ones of different shapes and sizes and carried them up to her room. There, in secret, she took the squares of felt from her dressing-up box and spread them out on the floor. Some squares were deep red, some dark orange and some golden yellow. Azra placed a leaf on each and carefully cut round the shape. She sat back to look at the result and was pleased with the felt leaves she had made. At this point her mum called up to her. Azra hid the leaves inside a jigsaw puzzle box and went downstairs.

The next day, again in secret, she stuck large red and orange felt leaves onto the long black scarf, overlapping them with each other to make interesting shapes. Finally, she stuck some of the smallest yellow felt leaves on top, to make a random pattern like the leaves in the garden.

Azra had been so absorbed in what she was doing, she hadn't realised how late it was. Quickly, before her mum could come upstairs to see what she was doing, she hid the scarf under her bed, waiting until the following day before she worked on the other side. This time she stuck some yellow leaves on first. When she added the red and orange ones, she made sure that, here and there along the length of the scarf, curvy slices of the golden yellow peeped out from under the darker red and orange. In an almost magical way, Azra seemed to know just where these golden glints wanted to be.

After she had stuck on the very last leaf, Azra lay the scarf along her bed and gazed at it with pleasure. She turned the scarf over. Each side had a different leafy pattern of autumn colour and Azra really couldn't decide which she liked best. She smiled, full to the brim with pleasure. It felt good to have made such a beautiful thing. She wrapped it up carefully.

On the morning of mum's birthday, Azra gave her the card she had made and the gift which dad had bought for her to give – lovely scented soap. Azra waited until the evening to give her very own present. Mum was in her new black coat, ready to go out with Dad. Grandma was there to look after Azra.

"I didn't manage to find a new scarf to go with my new coat," mum said to dad.

Azra and Grandma smiled at each other.

"Here's another birthday present I made all by myself mum," Azra said.

Surprised, mum opened the parcel and unfolded the scarf. She actually gasped. She gave Azra a hug and draped the scarf around her neck so that the lovely pattern of autumn colours stood out against the plain dark coat. The golden yellow almost glowed.

Dad and Grandma were smiling and Azra herself was smiling so hard that her cheeks began to ache.

Mum wasn't smiling though. With a look of wonder on her face she was gazing into the mirror and blinking tears of joy. "Thank you Azra," she said. "This is the loveliest gift I have ever, ever had.

4 TALKING ABOUT THE STORY

Did the children understand?

- What items did Azra keep for her dressing-up box?

- What did Azra's mum want to wear with her new black coat?

- How much money did Azra have to buy a present for her mum?

- Why did Azra not want to do an autumn painting?

- How did Azra make the scarf?

Points for discussion

- How did Azra make each side of the scarf different but interesting? This provides an opportunity for the children to grasp the idea of thinking/reflecting/being self-critical as we work. (Imagination plus critical/hard thought.)

- Discuss why Azra's mum was so moved by Azra's gift.

- Azra used her imagination to make her gift. Talk about imagination with the children.

- The story also provides an opportunity to talk about the different seasons of the year.

5 THE LEARNING ACTIVITY

Links

i) The activity links to the story through encouraging creativity with pattern, leaf shapes and autumn colours.

ii) The assembly connects with the story through valuing creativity and creation.

iii) If you wish to link the activity to the assembly the children's pictures could be displayed.

ACTIVITY SUGGESTIONS

- These activities involve working as an individual.

- The children will need: **1** a bag each for their leaves **2** either autumn-coloured thick card (red, gold, orange) and paper glue, or autumn-coloured felt (red, gold, orange) and fabric glue.

1 AUTUMN WALK

The children can be taken for an autumn walk to collect leaves. They should try to find a variety of colours, shapes and sizes.

2 AUTUMN COLLAGE

The children place the leaves on the coloured card or fabric and draw round the leaf shapes. The leaves may be softened with Vaseline if they are too dry and brittle to draw around. The children then cut out leaves of various colours, shapes and sizes. They stick their leaves onto their own sheet of paper, in overlapping patterns, to make their own autumn collage – a unique design.

Assembly

Theme: Creativity and Creation

Introduction

The assembly leader introduces the theme of creation; that all the world religions, in different ways, recognise and praise the creator of the universe. We are awed by the existence of this vast and beautiful creation. The assembly leader connects this with our own creative impulse. In striving to create beautiful and interesting things we experience fulfilment.

Story

Assembly leader:

"Our story today is about Azra, a girl who, using her imagination, makes a very special gift for her mother. She uses the beautiful colours and shapes of autumn leaves."

The assembly leader reads the story – *A Pattern of Pleasure*.

Poem or song

You can choose a poem or a song or both. Many hymns praise the creator and may still be appropriate in a multi-faith context. Select poems and songs which are relevant to the theme or which echo the story in some way.

Examples

Poems:

Crayoning (creating a picture)
Page 14 in *A Very First Poetry Book* by Stanley Cook, published by Oxford University Press, 1984.

I'm a Tree (highlights falling autumn leaves)
Page 93 in *Smile Please* by Tony Bradman, published by Puffin, 1989.

Songs:

Morning has Broken (praising creation)
No. 3 in *Someone's Singing Lord* (2nd Edition), published by A&C Black, 2002.

I Can Climb (self-expression)
No. 17 in *Every Colour Under the Sun*, published by Ward Lock Educational Co. Ltd., 1983.

Assembly visitor

Perhaps you could invite a local artist or writer to join the assembly to talk briefly about their work (show or read some) and to answer questions from the children.

Quiet reflection or prayer

For a universal, humanistic or multi-faith assembly:

Quiet reflection

The assembly leader says:
"We are full of wonder at the existence and beauty of the universe. Let us close our eyes and in our own words, thank the Creator. (Pause) When we create something ourselves we too want to make it as beautiful as we can. Let's think for a moment about that. (Pause) Azra used the colours and shapes of autumn leaves. Let us also pause to feel grateful for our world of colour." (Pause)

Or for Christian schools:

Prayer

Let us pray.

Almighty God,
Creator of the Universe, help us to be grateful for the wonders of your creation including the wonder of colour. Help us to develop our creativity, so that we may be blessed with the satisfaction of making beautiful things.

Amen.

Chapter 9

The Day the Sky Fell Down
Teacher's Notes

Theme Nine: The value of **Kindness/Compassion**

Values Education: Learning to act with kindness and
care is part of **Moral Education**

> Justice and compassion are the twin pillars of morality. A child who
> acts with loving kindness is exhibiting the crucial capacity for
> compassion – a capacity which must be stimulated and nurtured in
> moral and emotional education.

Lesson Plan

This five-part lesson plan is only a guide. Teachers are likely to add to or amend the learning activities which are suggested and may sometimes wish to substitute their own. For any part of the session they may wish to allow more or less time than that suggested.

1 Introduce the theme   *5–10 minutes*

What is **kindness/compassion**?
The teacher gives examples and explains why we should be kind.
The children add some examples of their own and talk about these.

2 Vocabulary   *5 minutes*

The teacher ensures that the children understand the words given.
This can be integrated into the reading of the story.

3 The story   *5–10 minutes*

The teacher shows the illustration and reads the story.

4 Talking about the story   *10–15 minutes*

The teacher uses some of the questions and discussion points given,
stimulating the children to talk about the story/theme.
Some of the questions could be integrated into the reading of the
story.

5 The learning activity   *20–35 minutes*

Learning about oxygen/labelling the bird.
Some suggested activities could be used in subsequent, follow-up
lessons.

Total time *45–75 minutes*

1 INTRODUCE THE THEME

Key points

- We all appreciate kindness shown to us.

- We cement good relations by being kind.

- It is easier to be kind when we feel compassion (perhaps link to empathy).

- To learn to act in a caring way is to become a good (better) person.

2 VOCABULARY

Use your usual methods for introducing new words.

The difficult words in the story are:

compassion	-	*sympathy, kindness, care, pity*
stretched	-	*pulled to make wider/longer*
agape	-	*wide open*
desperately	-	*despairingly, frantically*
cautiously	-	*very carefully*
dim	-	*very low light*
loomed	-	*suddenly towered over*
pounce	-	*spring on*
dazed	-	*confused*
cosy	-	*warm and snug*
musty	-	*stale, damp air; closed in*
curiously	-	*wanting to know about something*
imploringly	-	*beggingly*
fog	-	*thick mist*

3 THE STORY:

The Day the Sky Fell Down

Beady and his mum are grateful to Mr Owl for his kindness

The Day the Sky Fell Down

Beady stretched his wings, opened his eyes and with yellow beak agape, stared about in astonishment. He was surrounded by swirling grey clouds.

"Stone the crows!" he exclaimed. "The sky has fallen down."

The young blackbird was scared. He tried hard not to cry but the tears welled up anyway and soon he was weeping.

"Where's my mum?" he sobbed. "I want my mum."

Just then, a large black and white Magpie flew into view.

"Stop, please stop," Beady shouted, desperately.

But the Magpie flew on calling, "Sorry Beady. There's a meeting at the pond."

"A meeting," thought Beady. "About the sky! I bet that's where my mum is. I'll go and find her."

Beady flew into the thick clouds, where he soon got completely lost. On and on he flew through the endless grey sky until his small wings were achingly tired. He flew cautiously towards the ground for a rest. He landed, with an unpleasant bump, on a long, dark road. Dim lights grew brighter as a car loomed near and Beady hopped onto the pavement just in time. Almost immediately, a whiskery face with gleaming green eyes glared down at him.

Before the cat could pounce, Beady managed to launch himself back into the air, all thought of a rest forgotten. With his heart thudding hard in his chest, Beady flew on. And on. By now the small blackbird was terrified that he might never see his mum again. His heart ached as painfully as his wings. On and on he flew until he was so tired that he crashed into a tree. Beady fell, not too far, fortunately, and lay on his back, dazed. Two huge birds towered over him. It was Mr and Mrs Owl.

"Are you all right, little bird?" asked Mrs Owl kindly.

The two owls carried Beady up to a hole in the tree. Inside the hole there was a cosy room which smelled of musty, warm owls. There, three owl chicks repeating 'food please, food please' stopped to stare at Beady curiously. Mrs Owl gave Beady and the chicks some bread dipped in water.

"Why are you out on your own dear?" she asked.

"I'm looking for my mum," Beady told her. "She wasn't there when I woke up and now I'm lost."

"I expect she'll be back by now. Could you take him home, Dink?" she said to Mr Owl. "I must stay with the chicks you see."

"Brill," thought Beady, but to his dismay Mr Owl refused.

"I've got to finish my work," he grumbled, as he continued to write in a big book. "He'll find his own way home dear, later."

In the silence that followed, once more Beady blinked hard to keep back his tears. Mr Owl wrote for a while in the big book and then looked up. Beady stared at him imploringly. Mr Owl's serious face softened into a smile.

"Oh, all right lad," he said. "I'll take you home. Blackbird Copse, is it?"

Beady followed Mr Owl, staying close in the thick clouds. They soon reached Blackbird Copse and Beady's heart lifted, light as a feather, when he saw his own tree. Beady's mum was extremely relieved to see him.

"Thank you. Thank you, Mr Owl, so kind, so very kind," she said. "But wherever have you been, Beady?"

Beady realised that she sounded cross only because she had been extremely worried.

"Why didn't you stay in the nest like you usually do?"

"I didn't know what to do," Beady explained. "Because of the sky falling down."

Beady's mum and Mr Owl laughed and laughed.

"Beady this is fog," his mum said at last. "It's not the sky. It will clear up later, you'll see."

"A natural mistake," said kind Mr Owl. "After all, he's never seen fog before. In fact, Beady, it was rather a clever idea – the sky falling down."

Beady's mum and Mr Owl laughed again, but so kindly that Beady didn't mind. He was happy to have had an adventure and even more happy to be safe home with his mum.

"Say thank you to Mr Owl," she said to him, "for bringing you home."

"Thank you Mr Owl," Beady said. "Thank you very much indeed."

4 TALKING ABOUT THE STORY

Did the children understand?

- What surprised Beady when he woke up?

- Who told Beady about the meeting?

- What two things nearly hurt Beady?

- Who helped Beady?

- What made Mr Owl and Beady's mum laugh?

Points for discussion

- Discuss how we feel when someone is kind to us and why we sometimes want to be kind and why we should be kind (even, sometimes, when we don't want to be – like Mr Owl in the story).

- Discuss, too, why we should be kind to animals.

- In addition, this provides an opportunity to discuss with the children what they should do if they get lost.
  (Unlike in *The Bumblebee Man*, they may not only be lost at the shops.)

---

5 THE LEARNING ACTIVITY

Links

i)   The activity links to the story through its focus on birds.

ii) The assembly connects with the story through valuing kindness and care.

iii) If you wish to link the activity to the coming assembly, display the children's labelled birds, or a child might rehearse their animal story to read in the assembly. (Select one where the element of kindness is clearly there.)

ACTIVITY SUGGESTIONS

- These activities involve working as individuals and as a class.

- The children will need 'safe' scissors, glue, rulers and pens.

1 LABELLING A BIRD

Photocopy the bird page for each child. The children should carefully cut off the word list and then each separate word. They should then glue the bird onto the middle of a sheet of white paper.

Draw the simple bird outline on the black or whiteboard and label each part as shown below. The children should pick out the correct words and stick their labels onto their sheet, adding an arrow to label the correct parts of the bird. (This is an opportunity to learn some basic facts about birds and to learn and recognise some associated vocabulary.)

2 UNDERSTANDING BIRDS

Explain that the wings enable the bird to fly. Explain about migration.

3 RECOGNISING BIRDS

Use some pictures of common birds (owl, blackbird, magpie, robin etc.) and teach the children how to recognise them.

4 CLASS VISIT

Try putting wet bread and unsalted nuts outside, in sight of the classroom window, so that the children can watch as the birds come to feed.

It may be possible to arrange a class outing to visit a park or zoo with an aviary.

5 STORY OR PICTURES

Younger children could draw a picture of an act of kindness to a person or a pet. Older children could write a story about a creature (a pet or a wild creature) incorporating a kind act – as in *The Day the Sky Fell Down*.

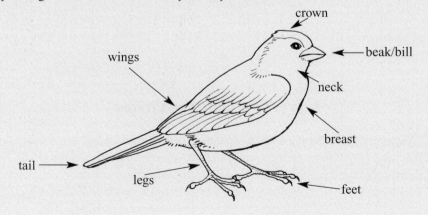

TAIL

NECK

BREAST

WINGS

FEET

LEGS

CROWN

BEAK/BILL

cut

Assembly

Theme: Kindness and Care

Introduction

The assembly leader introduces the theme and talks about why we value kindness and therefore why we should be kind. It is especially easy to be kind to those we care about but we should be kind to others too – like Mr Owl in the story. Understanding/feeling sorry for someone often helps us to be kind.

Story

Assembly leader:

"Our story today is about a small blackbird who was lost and then found."

The assembly leader reads the story – *The Day the Sky Fell Down*.

Getting lost (again)

The assembly leader could take the opportunity to reinforce the messages about what to do if you get lost.

Poem or song

You can choose a poem or a song or both. Select poems and songs which are relevant to the theme or which echo the story in some way.

Examples

Poems:

Robin (kindness to the robin redbreast)
Page 116 in *A Very First Poetry Book* by Iain Crichton Smith, published by Oxford University Press, 1984.

A Good Idea for Wintry Weather (kindness to dad)
Page 112 in *A Very First Poetry Book* by Libby Houston, published by Oxford University Press, 1984.

Songs:

Jesus' Hands were Kind Hands (the value of kindness)
No. 33 in *Someone's Singing Lord* (2nd Edition), published by A&C Black, 2002.

Take Care of a Friend (kindness and compassion)
No. 35 in *Every Colour Under the Sun*, published by Ward Lock Educational Co. Ltd., 1983.

Quiet reflection or prayer

For a universal, humanistic or multi-faith assembly:

Quiet reflection

The assembly leader says:
"Let us be thankful for those who are kind to us. (Pause) Let us try to be kind too. Let us think, now, of ways we can be kind to our family and our friends today." (Pause)

Or for Christian schools:

Prayer

Let us pray.

Lord God,
Help us to be kind and caring to others as you are kind and caring to us and all of your creatures. Bless and guide all those who care for others in the work they do – nurses, doctors, parents, care workers and teachers.

Amen.

Chapter 10

A Secret Place

Teacher's Notes

Theme Ten: The value of **Appreciation of the Natural World**

Values Education: Learning to be appreciate the Natural World is part of **Spiritual Education**

> Appreciation of the natural world is part of spiritual education in several ways: gratitude to the creator; wonder at the fact of creation; appreciation of its amazing beauty, mystery and diversity; transcendence of self in contemplating that beauty/mystery.

Lesson Plan

This five-part lesson plan is only a guide. Teachers are likely to add to or amend the learning activities which are suggested and may sometimes wish to substitute their own. For any part of the session they may wish to allow more or less time than that suggested.

1 Introduce the theme *5–10 minutes*

What do we mean by **appreciation**?
What do we mean by the **natural world**?
Why do we appreciate the natural world? (Its beauty, its fascination, the joy it can give to us.) Give examples.

2 Vocabulary *5 minutes*

The teacher ensures that the children understand the words given. This can be integrated into the reading of the story.

3 The story *5–10 minutes*

The teacher shows the illustration and reads the story.

4 Talking about the story *10–15 minutes*

The teacher uses some of the questions and discussion points given, stimulating the children to talk about the story/theme.
Some of the questions could be integrated into the reading of the story.

5 The learning activity *20–35 minutes*

The class enjoys a nature walk and create (or add to) a class nature table. They write a 'recipe' poem. Some suggested activities could be used in subsequent, follow-up lessons.

Total time | *45–75 minutes*

1 INTRODUCE THE THEME

Key points

● The children need to think first about all the wonders of the natural world – oceans, mountains, trees, flowers, creatures, etc.

● The children should consciously reflect on the joy and pleasure all these things add to our lives.

2 VOCABULARY

Use your usual methods for introducing new words.

The difficult words in the story are:

appreciation	-	*valuing something and recognising its true worth; being grateful for something*
natural world	-	*the unspoiled world – the countryside (mountains, fields, sea, sky and the creatures that live there)*
irritated	-	*annoyed*
sturdy	-	*strong*
meadow	-	*natural field, piece of grassland*
enclosed	-	*surrounded by a barrier of some sort, without a gap*
solid	-	*impenetrable, like a stone*
frustration	-	*strong dissatisfaction felt when prevented from doing something*
peaceful	-	*quiet and harmonious, calm*

3 THE STORY:

A Secret Place

Oscar marvelled at how beautiful it was

A Secret Place

Oscar missed his friends from the city, especially as he had no brothers or sisters to play with. At the old house he had played in the square with loads of other kids – football, scooters, marbles, cricket – all sorts of exciting games, one after the other, all day long.

"Why don't you go out and play?" said his mum, who was irritated by his grumbles, though she understood too, and was sorry.

"Look Oscar," she said, "once you start at your new school and make new friends you can bring them home to play. Now, out you go."

Oscar went out into the garden where he gazed round for something to do. He ran to a tall tree which had good, sturdy branches, and climbed right to the top. High up in the tree Oscar could see beyond his own garden, into a small meadow nearby. This was completely enclosed by high hedges, which made it seem like an unknown, secret place. An exciting hidden place. He saw an old barn and he spotted a stream for jumping. He climbed down the tree as quickly as he could and ran to the very end of the long garden, hoping to find a way into the field. To his disappointment, Oscar found that a tall wooden fence ran the whole length of the bottom edge of his garden, right up to the thick, high hedges growing down each side. The fence was straight and solid and it was certainly too high to climb.

Oscar sighed in frustration, but, as he stood in front of the fence longing to get into the field, he sensed that he was being watched. He turned, and saw two bright green eyes, the eyes of a cat, staring at him from a gap at the bottom of the hedge. The creature turned and disappeared.

Curiously, Oscar bent low and pushed his way through the gap. The hedge was thick and green with a low open space running through the middle. Oscar followed the cat. He had to crouch down to fit through the low space. Slowly he pushed his way along, foot by foot. Twice he was scratched by the hedge but soon another gap opened up and Oscar pushed his way out. The low tunnel in the thick hedge had brought him into the unreachable field. "Yes!" he shouted, punching the air in delight.

Oscar walked all round the small field. It was, indeed, completely enclosed by thick hedges, and, on one side, by his own high garden fence. Oscar enjoyed exploring, though at one point a grass snake gave him a shock before it slithered away. A little later, he entered the old barn. It was dark inside, and he was a bit nervous, but when his eyes adjusted he could see that it would make a brilliant den. Finally, he explored the swiftly flowing stream. He saw fish in there, and on a stone in the water, a frog which was completely unafraid of him. It sat on its stone and croaked.

Oscar returned to the gap in the hedge, but before leaving he had a final look round, and marvelled at how beautiful it was. Tall grasses waved gently in the breeze, threaded through with white and yellow wild flowers. The stream glinted like a silver snake in the sunshine. There were masses of butterflies – small white and yellow ones which matched the flowers and big black and orange ones too. It was very peaceful. The only sound was the song of birds. The bright blue sky was like a ceiling for a secret outdoor room.

"It's paradise," thought Oscar. He gazed and gazed, full of amazement to have discovered such a secret and beautiful place. Then, as he stood looking, a fox appeared with her two cubs. The cubs were running round each other – playing like puppies. Suddenly the mother fox saw Oscar. For a magical moment they stared at each other. Oscar was not afraid.

With light, bright eyes the fox gazed at him before she turned and ran, her cubs following. Oscar watched, holding his breath until they had gone. He gave a long sigh of pure joy.

Eventually, he pushed his way into the hedge again, and crouched his way back to his garden. No one knew that he had been away.

The next day, Oscar carved his name on a piece of wood and nailed it on the old barn door. He asked his mum for three small but strong boxes which had been used in the furniture removal. It was hard work pushing these through the tunnel in the hedge but they made a great table and chairs for his barn den. He didn't tell his mum and dad about the wild garden beyond their own. He had decided that he would keep it as a secret garden to share only with whoever became his best friend at the new school.

4 TALKING ABOUT THE STORY

Did the children understand?

- Why did Oscar have no friends?

- How did Oscar get into the enclosed meadow?

- What four kinds of creatures did Oscar see in the meadow?

- What kind of creatures did he hear?

- What did Oscar nail to the old barn door?

Points for discussion

- Why was the meadow so special? You can discuss its natural beauty, its peace and solitude, its secret, hidden quality and Oscar's plan to share it with a best/special friend.

- What things/places do the children find special? And why?

- You can discuss the huge variety of interesting creatures in the world (biodiversity) and explore the delight of seeing wild creatures in their own habitat, like Oscar saw the fox. What wild creatures do the children like? And why?

5 THE LEARNING ACTIVITY

Links

i)   The activity links to the story through a focus on nature.

ii) The assembly connects with the story through valuing the appreciation of the natural world.

iii) If you wish to link the activity to the coming assembly you could set up a nature table in the assembly hall, and select some of the children's poems to be read.

ACTIVITY SUGGESTIONS

- These activities involve working as a whole class and as individuals.

- The children will need (ideally) a small bag each in which to put their finds, and you will need a (small) table for the nature display.

I A NATURE WALK

Talk about what the children are likely to find on their nature walk, even if it is only possible to walk round the school playing field. For example, different kinds of leaves, twigs, stones, conkers, berries, grasses, wild flowers.

2 A NATURE TABLE

You may already have a nature table. In this case you can add the best of the children's finds. If you do not already have one, this is an opportunity to create one. (You could ask children to begin to bring in natural objects a few weeks before this session – and to continue to do so after it.)

Older children could write out appropriate labels.

3 A NATURE POEM

The natural world makes a good theme for a poem. You could read some of the many nature poems and help the children to write a poem about things they like to see – butterflies, flowers, birds, the sea, etc. This could be done as a *recipe* poem for their own 'secret garden'. (The poem needn't rhyme, of course.)
Example:

Secret Garden

Take a whole bag of creatures
A cupful of flowers
Add a teaspoon of butterflies
Sunshine and showers.
A pinch of peace
And one good friend
Bake a beautiful garden
To love and to tend.

Younger children could write a 'sense' poem:

I can smell the flowers
I can see the colours
I can hear the bees buzzing
I can feel the soft, furry leaves.

4 DRAWING A PICTURE

The children could draw a picture of somewhere that is a special place to them.

Assembly

Theme: Appreciation of the Natural World

Introduction

The assembly leader introduces the theme and talks about the things we appreciate in the natural world and the joy they give to us. This can be linked to the notion of wonder at creation and gratitude to the creator.

Story

Assembly leader:

"Our story today is about Oscar, a boy who discovered the joy and beauty of the natural world. In solitude we often experience the wonder and richness of this beauty."

The assembly leader reads the story – *A Secret Place*.

Poem or song

You can choose a poem or a song or both or some of the children could read their own nature poems. Select poems and songs which are relevant to the theme or which echo the story in some way.

Examples

Poems:

Up on the Downs (celebration of nature)
Page 67 in *A Very First Poetry Book* by Wes Magee, published by Oxford University Press, 1984.

Spring Song (celebration of spring)
Page 117 in *A Very First Poetry Book* by Jean Kenward, published by Oxford University Press, 1984.

Songs:

I Love the Sun (appreciation of the natural world and its creator)
No. 12 in *Someone's Singing Lord* (2nd Edition), published by A&C Black, 2002.

Give to us eyes (to appreciate the beautiful world)
No. 18 in *Someone's Singing Lord* (2nd Edition), published by A&C Black, 2002.

The World is Such a Lovely Place (appreciation of the world)
No. 8 in *Every Colour Under the Sun*, published by Ward Lock Educational Co. Ltd., 1983.

Quiet reflection or prayer

For a universal, humanistic or multi-faith assembly:

Quiet reflection

The assembly leader says:
"Close your eyes and picture the following:
The crashing waves of the sea. (Pause) A beautiful field like Oscars' meadow. (Pause) A beautiful wild creature such as a tiger or an elephant. (Pause) Let us feel glad that we live in such a beautiful world. (Pause) Let us remember to treat this world with appreciation and care. (Pause) In your own words you can say thank you to the Creator." (Pause)

Or for Christian schools:

Prayer

Let us pray.

Dear God,
Creator of the world, open our eyes to the full wonder and beauty of the world in which we live. Help us to appreciate and to look after this world and the wild creatures.

Amen.

Chapter 11

Confident as Chloe

Teacher's Notes

Theme Eleven: The value of **Self-confidence**

Values Education: Learning to be self-confident is part of **Personal Education**

> Teachers and parents recognise that children need to become self-confident. On this one characteristic depends much of their well-being away from home and their ability to form new relationships. Thus their success in school and in later life is correlated with their level of self-confidence. The development of self-confidence requires the development of a positive self-concept. Each child needs to experience success and to learn to accept themselves, their strengths and weaknesses.

Lesson Plan

This five-part lesson plan is only a guide. Teachers are likely to add to or amend the learning activities which are suggested and may sometimes wish to substitute their own. For any part of the session they may wish to allow more or less time than that suggested.

1 Introduce the theme *5–10 minutes*

What is **self-confidence**?
The teacher gives examples and distinguishes self-confidence from vanity/arrogance.
The children add some examples of their own and talk about these.

2 Vocabulary *5 minutes*

The teacher ensures that the children understand the words given. This can be integrated into the reading of the story.

3 The story *5–10 minutes*

The teacher shows the illustration and reads the story.

4 Talking about the story *10–15 minutes*

The teacher uses some of the questions and discussion points given, stimulating the children to talk about the story/theme. Some of the questions could be integrated into the reading of the story.

5 The learning activity *20–35 minutes*

Working in pairs, the children explore their own strengths, followed by a 'division' exercise. Some suggested activities could be used in subsequent, follow-up lessons.

| **Total time** | *45–75 minutes* |

1 INTRODUCE THE THEME

Key points

What is 'self-confidence'? Contrast with shyness and low self-esteem, but also with self-conceit and vanity. Ask – have you ever felt shy? What can we do if we feel shy? What can we do to help someone else who feels shy?

Explain the value of self-confidence/assertiveness against bullying.

Give examples of self-confidence – such as speaking up for oneself, knowing your good points and skills, being able to speak/read/dance/act, etc. in public.

Lead the children into giving some examples and talk with the class about these.

2 VOCABULARY

Use your usual methods for introducing new words.

The difficult words in the story are:

self-confidence	-	*self-esteem – belief in one's ability and character*
fair	-	*just*
argumentative	-	*quarrelsome*
scalding	-	*burning hot*
nickname	-	*pet name, often a shortened version of their proper name*
reared up	-	*(a horse) standing up on two legs*
concentration	-	*giving full attention*
in spite of	-	*despite/even though ...*
efforts	-	*tries/attempts*
conceited	-	*vain*

3 THE STORY:

Confident as Chloe

Chloe learned to be more self-confident

Confident as Chloe

Pippa is a great nickname. It sounds like birdsong. Pippa – Pippa. Unfortunately, it reminded Pippa Taylor of the pips of an orange. Being pale and small for her age, with bright orange-red hair too, she hated this idea – Pippa, pips, orange pip – ugh! Fortunately, one cold Monday last year, Pippa got the chance to change her name. It was one good thing which came out of several bad ones.

The bad things began one morning, at breakfast, when, lost in a dream, Pippa was sipping very hot tea just as her brother yelled so loudly that she jumped, scalding her mouth. Ouch!

"S'not fair," yelled John.

"I got it first," Eddie bellowed back.

The twins were quarrelling, as usual. This time over the last piece of hot, buttery toast. Unlike Pippa, who was quiet and shy, her twin brothers were noisy and argumentative.

After breakfast, the twins went to play at their friend's house, but Pippa had no one to play with.

"You'll have to come with me to the McGreggors," said her mum. Pippa's heart sank.

"Do I have to mum?" she said. Pippa was secretly a bit frightened of Mrs McGreggor.

"You can't stay here on your own love," said mum.

The McGreggors lived in a big house with a huge garden. Twice a week, Mrs Taylor, Pippa's mum, went there to clean and polish.

"Can I help?" Pippa asked, as her mother lifted out the vacuum from a cupboard under the stairs.

"You could do the polishing, love. Like you sometimes do at home. Just a little polish and a lot of rub."

Her mum gave Pippa a tin of polish and a yellow duster. Pippa started with the table in the hall. First she polished the legs. They were carved and curvy and took a long time. As she rubbed them clean, Pippa was thinking about her own name. Phillipa, Penelope, Chloe Taylor. Her nickname, 'Pippa', was short for 'Phillipa'. Pippa had never complained about her nickname, not even to her mum. Like cold days, she thought, as she finished the table legs, it was just one of those things you have to put up with.

A delicate china horse stood on top of the table; it reared up on two legs and its pale white was reflected in the dark polished wood. Seeing how lovely he was, Pippa lifted him higher for a closer look. She was smiling at him with pleasure when, somehow, he slipped from her fingers and smashed into pieces on the tiled floor. In the deep silence that followed, she gazed down in horror at what she had done. She felt herself turn hot and trembly. Mrs McGreggor and her mum ran into the hall. Her mum gave a gasp of dismay and her hand flew up to her mouth.

"My lovely horse," said Mrs McGreggor. "You clumsy girl. No more dusting. Out you go. You can wait for your mum in the garden. At least there's no expensive china out there."

"I'm s… so s… sorry," stuttered Pippa quietly, but Mrs McGreggor, ignoring this, opened the door and waited for her to go outside. Pippa slunk past, head down, and as the door slammed behind her, she felt the cold air on her cheeks, and the hot tears spilling down.

As she was crying, the door opened again, and her mum was there.

"Put this on, it's cold." She handed over Pippa's coat and seeing the tears she said,

"Don't cry love. You didn't mean to do it. Look, sit on that bench over there and I'll be as quick as I can and then we'll go home."

Pippa sat on the bench. She cried for so long that by the time her mum came out again she had no tears left to cry, but she was very, very cold.

"Ready love?" her mum called.

Pippa was pleased to be going home but even on the way back another horrid thing occurred. Further down the road the McGreggor boys were playing and one of them shouted:

"You broke our horse Pippa Taylor."

"Pippa the pipsqueak," shouted the other.

They began to follow, chanting "Pippa pipsqueak, orange pips, Pippa pipsqueak orange pips," until Mrs Taylor turned round and told them, very firmly indeed, to go home at once.

"What's a pipsqueak, mum?" Pippa asked.

"Someone unimportant love. Not like you. You're very important," and mum gave her hand a squeeze.

"Take no notice of those rude boys. Remember what Granny always says? Sticks and stones may break your bones but names will never hurt you."

Pippa said nothing, but she knew that Granny was wrong. She did feel hurt.

Back home again Pippa curled up by the fire and lost herself in reading a story about King Solomon, all her hurt feelings forgotten. Meanwhile, mum was cooking in the kitchen, and as soon as the twins came home they all sat down to eat their tea. This time the twins quarrelled about who should have the last coconut cake.

"You had more chips than me," John said.

"You had extra cake last night," Eddie shouted, enraged.

Pippa saw how tired her mum looked. She was slumped at the table, her head on one hand. Her face was pale and her drooping eyes were ringed with dark shadows.

"I wish they would just shut up," Pippa thought. Suddenly, she had an idea.

"Let John cut and Eddie choose," Pippa said.

After a brief frown, mum's tired face lit up in a big smile.

"Goodness, Pippa, I do believe that would work!"

She put the plate with the last coconut cake in front of John.

"Be careful with the knife," she said, as she handed it to him.

"Now John, you cut and you, Eddie, you choose the first piece."

John took the knife, and, as they all watched, very carefully, with the utmost concentration, he divided the cake into two. He tried to cut it exactly in half, but in spite of his efforts, one piece was slightly bigger. Eddie chose that piece of course. John didn't argue though. After all, he had done the cutting. Their quarrel forgotten, the twins ate the cake.

Pippa's mum smiled at her.

"Phillipa, Penelope, Chloe Taylor," she said, "you should just have been called 'clever Chloe'.

"Chloe would do," said Pippa. "I wish people would just call me Chloe."

"Right," said mum, and she told the twins they must call their sister 'Chloe' from now on.

And the next day, she had a word with Chloe's teacher. At first the children at school sometimes forgot, but soon no one remembered that Chloe had ever been called anything else.

And ever since that day, mealtimes have been peaceful in the Taylor family. The twins take it in turns – one cuts and the other chooses. Chloe herself has become less shy. She knows now that she can sometimes have really good ideas. If she feels nervous she asks herself, "What would clever Chloe do?" And without it making her in the least bit conceited, Chloe's confidence grows and grows.

4 TALKING ABOUT THE STORY

Did the children understand?

- Why did Pippa not like her nickname?

- What did Pippa's brothers first quarrel about?

- Why did Pippa not want to go to the McGreggors?

- What did Pippa break?

- What new name did Pippa choose?

Points for discussion

- Discuss the difference between doing something by accident (as Pippa did when she broke the horse) and doing something deliberately.
  (We are less to blame when we do something by accident, though we should try to take care not to – especially with other people's things.) You could also discuss Mrs McGreggor's hard reaction.

- Discuss the importance of names, and the badness of name-calling, which is a form of bullying. What should you do about name-calling?

- Discuss ways in which we can learn to be more self-confident and assertive. What did Chloe do, in the end, to help herself to feel confident? (She reminds herself of 'clever Chloe' who had such a good idea and asks herself what clever Chloe would do.)

5 THE LEARNING ACTIVITY

Links

i) The activity links to the story through both exercises – a self-confidence one and a sharing one.

ii) The assembly connects with the story through valuing self-confidence and denouncing bullying.

iii) If you wish to link the activity to the coming assembly, four of the children could read a half page each of the story – *Confident as Chloe*.

ACTIVITY SUGGESTIONS

- These activities involve working as a whole class and also in pairs.

- The children will need two small pieces of fruit and one 'safe' knife per pair of children.

1 SELF-ESTEEM ACTIVITY

With the children in a circle, ask each child to say one good thing about themselves. For example:

'Sometimes I help my mum by …'
'Once I was very brave when I went to the dentist.'

Go round again and ask them to say one good thing about another person. For example:

'X is a friendly person.'
'X is good at reading.'
'I like Ann's new shoes.'

The teacher could also take a turn – in saying a good thing about *each* child (thus no one is left out).

And/or:

Divide the children into pairs. Each child should tell the other at least three good things about themselves. Each child should tell the other at least three good things about the other.

2 DIVISION EXERCISE

This is to reinforce that *one* thing divides into *two* halves.

Give each pair of children two pieces of fruit, (e.g. one banana, one soft pear.)

The two children each cut one of the pieces of fruit in half. The other child chooses which 'half' to have (as in the story).

3 THE WISDOM OF SOLOMON

You could also tell the famous story of King Solomon, about cutting a baby in half, and enable the children to understand the King's wisdom, which is based, of course, on an understanding of maternal love.

Assembly

Theme: Self-confidence

Introduction

The assembly leader introduces the theme, and distinguishes between self-confidence and self-conceit. Assertiveness can help us against bullying, including name-calling, directed against us or against another. S/he can explain how bullying is a sign of insecurity, *not* of self-confidence.

Story

Assembly leader:

"Our story today is about how a girl's self-confidence grew stronger."

The assembly leader reads the story – *Confident as Chloe*.

The assembly leader could take the opportunity to talk about *bullying* and how to deal with it.

Poem or song

You can choose a poem or a song or both. Select poems and songs which are relevant to the theme or which echo the story in some way.

Examples

Poems:

The Name Game (the power of names – as in the story)
Page 88 in *Smile Please* by Tony Bradman, published by Puffin, 1989.

Picking Teams (destroying confidence)
Page 35 in *Please Mrs Butler* by Allan Ahlberg, published by Puffin, 1984.

Songs:

Lord, I Love to Stamp and Shout (celebration of what I am/will be)
No. 5 in *Someone's Singing Lord* (2nd Edition), published by A&C Black, 2002.

I Can Climb (having self-esteem)
No. 17 in *Every Colour Under the Sun*, published by Ward Lock Educational Co. Ltd., 1983.

Quiet reflection or prayer

For a universal, humanistic or multi-faith assembly:

Quiet reflection

The assembly leader says:
"Think about things you have learned to do and about good things you have done. (Pause) You feel pleased about these things. Think about good things you could do and decide to try to do these too. (Pause) If you have been a bully try to understand why you did this. (Pause) Think about how you feel when you are bullied. (Pause) Promise yourself that you will not bully again. (Pause) This is a good promise that you have made. And those of you who have been bullied, remember that it is not your fault. Think about telling me or your teacher about it. (Pause)

Or for Christian schools:

Prayer

Let us pray.

Dear God,
Help each one of us to grow in confidence but not in conceit. Help us not to bully and to stand up for those who are bullied, looking after those weaker than ourselves.

Amen.

Chapter 12

New Colours

Teacher's Notes

Theme Twelve: The value of **Friendship**

Values Education: Learning to make friends is part of
                     Social Education

> Having friends to play with is important to children, and the ability
> to make friends is of lifelong importance. Developing these
> friendship skills is thus a key part of social education. Learning to
> be friendly to new or lonely children and not to bully is, of course,
> also an important contribution to their moral development.

Lesson Plan

This five-part lesson plan is only a guide. Teachers are likely to add to or amend the learning activities which are suggested and may sometimes wish to substitute their own. For any
part of the session they may wish to allow more or less time than that suggested.

1   Introduce the theme   *5–10 minutes*

What is **friendship**?
Why is it important to us?
The teacher gives examples of what friends do with and for each other.
The children add some examples of their own and talk about these.

2   Vocabulary   *5 minutes*

The teacher ensures that the children understand the words given. This
can be integrated into the reading of the story.

3   The story   *5–10 minutes*

The teacher shows the illustration and reads the story.

4   Talking about the story   *10–15 minutes*

The teacher uses some of the questions and discussion points given,
stimulating the children to talk about the story/theme. Some of the
questions could be integrated into the reading of the story.

5   The learning activity   *20–35 minutes*

The children learn to mix new paint colours and paint a picture of
their best friend or an imaginary friend. Some suggested activities
could be used in subsequent, follow-up lessons.

Total time *45–75 minutes*

1 INTRODUCE THE THEME

Key points

Introduce the theme and talk about why we all need friends – the value of friendship and of being friendly. Who is your best friend? How do you make a friend? What makes a good friend?

Sometimes we move house or school and have to make new friends. Encourage the children to think of ways they can be welcoming to new children, such as showing them where the toilets are, inviting them to join in the play at playtime, talking to them and offering to be their partner when the teacher joins children into pairs.

2 VOCABULARY

Use your usual methods for introducing new words.

The difficult words in the story are:

friendship	-	*(state of) being friends*
friend	-	*someone you know well, with affection and trust between you*
summoned	-	*called to come*
peacock	-	*a bird with a wonderfully coloured tail*
murmur	-	*soft speaking/almost a whisper*
shades	-	*different strengths of the same colour*
blossoms	-	*flower heads*
carnival	-	*big street procession and party*
spectators	-	*watchers*
gorgeous	-	*lovely, splendid, dazzling*

3 THE STORY:

New Colours

Ruby and Katie paint together and learn to be friends

New Colours

Last Sunday Ruby's mum and dad moved to a new house and on Monday morning Ruby had to start at a new school. On the way there, clutching her mum's hand, she said: "I don't want to go mum. I want to stay at my old school with Alice." Alice was Ruby's best friend.

"I know love. But it's too far away now. Cheer up. You'll soon make new friends. You'll see."

At the new school mum said goodbye, and, left by herself in a room full of noisy, unknown children, Ruby blinked hard to hold back her tears. Miss Williams, the new teacher, put an arm round Ruby's shoulders. "Children," she said, "This is Ruby. You must help her to feel welcome." To Ruby she added, "This is your place dear, by Katie." Katie smiled at Ruby, but Ruby forgot to smile back. Shrugging, Katie turned away.

Miss Williams asked the children to sit in a circle.

"I want you to tell Ruby your name, and then to name one thing you really like. You start Billy."

"My name is William Dover, and I like …" Billy paused to think, "… I like football."

The boy on Billy's right went next.

"I'm Harry and I like … chocolate ice-cream." For some reason this made the children laugh.

"My name is Anita Bhalla, and I like computer games."

Soon it came round to Katie's turn.

"My name is Katie Gill and I like stories."

With the circle complete, Miss Williams turned to Ruby.

"Ruby, would you like to tell us one of your favourite things?"

Poor Ruby couldn't think of a single thing to say and as everyone waited, she felt her face go hot.

"Never mind dear," Miss Williams said. "My name is Miss Williams, and I like …" she paused and looked slowly round the circle of faces "… each of you."

At lunchtime Ruby had no one to play with. Alone and shivering in the cold playground she was glad when the school bell summoned everyone inside. Back in the classroom, Miss Williams asked Ruby and Katie to paint a garden of flowers.

"Oh bother, there's no green left," said Katie to Ruby. "How can we do a garden without any green?"

Anita, at the next table, said, "We need green too. For our peacock."

A murmur of dismay went round the classroom.

"Listen children," said Miss Williams. "We're out of green but …"

Ruby put up her hand.

"Yes Ruby," Miss Williams said, kindly.

"I know how to make green Miss."

"Know how to make green," said Katie. "You can't make green when there's no green paint, silly."

"Well, we'll see," said Miss Williams. "Gather round Ruby's table everyone."

Of course the children did so, but Ruby could see from their faces that they didn't believe her. Carefully Ruby took a big blob of blue paint and, as everybody watched, added a big blob of yellow. As soon as the blue and yellow blobs merged together, they changed to green.

"Wow," said the children.

"Magic," said Katie. She smiled at Ruby and Ruby smiled back.

"Well done Ruby," said Miss Williams. "Now does anyone know how to make purple?"

For a while Miss Williams showed the children how to mix new colours. Red and blue made purple, while red and yellow made orange. "It really is like magic," thought Ruby. By the time that the children went off to their painting again, Ruby and Katie's table was covered in jars with many shades of colours. Flower by flower they painted their garden.

When the garden was finished, green grass glowing with red, orange, purple and yellow blossoms, the two girls stood together and admired it. Ruby was happy that Katie was pleased. They had to wait until the painting was dry and then Miss Williams showed them exactly where to glue it onto a huge piece of white card, hanging ready on the wall.

Ruby and Katie's painting was the first to go on the big card. Gradually the other children added pictures too and when the final two children glued theirs into the last remaining gap, Ruby stared with pleasure at the completed scene – a street carnival, full of life. Ruby saw decorated lorries, food stalls, painted people in bright costumes, dancers, musicians and spectators. There was one house in the picture - a house with their garden.

The afternoon had whizzed by. Ruby was surprised to see mums and dads arriving already. She spotted her own mother.

"Mum, this is my new friend, Katie. Look, we did the garden."

"Hi Katie," smiled Ruby's mum. She looked at the garden in the bottom right-hand corner of the painting on the wall.

"What gorgeous colours," she said.

4 TALKING ABOUT THE STORY

Did the children understand?

- Why did Ruby have to go to a new school?

- What were some of the children's favourite things?

- What did Ruby and Katie paint?

- How did Ruby make green paint?

- What did all the children's paintings finally picture?

Points for discussion

- **Friends**
  How do we feel when we have no friends or no one to play with? What enjoyable things can we do on our own?

- How can we be friendly and welcoming to new children?
  (If any children have been 'new' kids they could say what was good and bad about their experience.)
  What makes a good friend? How do you make a new friend? Who is your best friend?

- **Colours**
  In addition, you could focus on colour.

  How did Miss Williams make purple and orange?
  What is your favourite colour?
  What would it be like not to see colours?
  What things have beautiful colours?
  (e.g. from other stories – tropical fish, birds, butterflies, flowers, autumn leaves.)

5 THE LEARNING ACTIVITY

Links

i)   The activity links to the story because of the theme of the paintings and the mixing of the new colours.

ii) The assembly connects with the story through the valuing of friendship.

iii) If you wish to link the activity to the assembly you could display the children's paintings of friends, and/or enact the role play about welcoming a new child.

ACTIVITY SUGGESTIONS

- The activities involve working as individuals or in pairs, and also in groups.
- The children will need white, red, blue and yellow paint.

1 PAINTING OF FRIENDS

The children are to paint their own picture on the theme of 'friends'. This could be a portrait of a best friend or an imaginary friend. It could be a picture of two friends playing or working together.

The children should be given only white, red, blue and yellow paint. From these they can mix:

blue + yellow = green
red + blue   = purple
red + yellow   = orange
white + red   = pink
blue + green   = turquoise
all the colours = brown

(Or the children could be asked to choose a partner and each paint the other's picture to give to them. However, this may not be a good idea if some children are likely to be missed out as a chosen friend.)

2 ROLE PLAY

After more discussion about what to do and what not to do to be welcoming to a new child in the class, the children could role play the arrival of a 'new' pupil. The role play should be of a good, welcoming class.

(They could do this as a whole group or in smaller groups of four.)

Assembly

Theme: Friendship

Introduction

The assembly leader introduces the theme and talks about why we need friends and why we should be friendly and welcoming to new children. Making friends brings a new relationship into being – s/he could use the analogy of mixing two colours to produce a new one.

Story

Assembly leader:

"Our story today is about Ruby, and what happens when she goes to a new school. It is about making someone new feel welcome and about making friends."

The assembly leader reads the story – *New Colours*.

Poem or song

You can choose a poem or a song or both or the children could enact their 'welcoming class' role play. Select poems and songs which are relevant to the theme or which echo the story in some way.

Examples

Poems:

I Had No Friends At All (the importance of a friend)
Page 18 in *A Very First Poetry Book* by John Kitching, published by Oxford University Press, 1984.

It is a Puzzle (the nature of friendship)
Page 48 in *Please Mrs Butler* by Allan Ahlberg, published by Puffin, 1984.

Songs:

Look Out for Loneliness (the value of friendship)
No. 36 in *Someone's Singing Lord* (2nd Edition), published by A&C Black, 2002.

Think of a World Without any Flowers (gratitude for good things, including friends)
No. 15 in *Someone's Singing Lord* (2nd Edition), published by A&C Black, 2002.

Take Care of a Friend (friendship and caring)
No. 35 in *Every Colour Under the Sun*, published by Ward Lock Educational Co. Ltd., 1983.

Quiet reflection or prayer

For a universal, humanistic or multi-faith assembly:

Quiet reflection

The assembly leader says:
"Let us think lovingly about our friends and be thankful for them. (Pause) Remembering how important friendship is, we can decide to try to be a good friend. (Pause) Let us think of any children who may be feeling lonely, and about how we could be friendly towards them. (Pause) Let us think about being welcoming to new children and teachers." (Pause)

Or for Christian schools:

Prayer

Let us pray.

Dear God,
Thank you for our friends. Help us to be a good friend to them and help us to be friendly to those who are lonely and to be welcoming to children and teachers who are new to the school.
Amen.

Chapter 13

Flashing Blue Light

Teacher's Notes

Theme Thirteen: The value of **Love**

Values Education: Learning to be loving is part of our **Emotional Development/Education**

> 'Faith, hope and love. And the greatest of these is love.' Goodness and love are two sides of the same coin. Thus love is the central value in our moral and emotional development.

Lesson Plan

This five-part lesson plan is only a guide. Teachers are likely to add to or amend the learning activities which are suggested and may sometimes wish to substitute their own. For any part of the session they may wish to allow more or less time than that suggested.

1 Introduce the theme   *5–10 minutes*

What is **love**?
The teacher explains the central importance of love – the link to so much else we value. Kindness, courage, pity, forgiveness, etc.
The teacher gives examples of acting lovingly.
The children add some examples of their own and talk about these.

2 Vocabulary   *5 minutes*

The teacher ensures that the children understand the words given.
This can be integrated into the reading of the story.

3 The story   *5–10 minutes*

The teacher shows the illustration and reads the story.

4 Talking about the story   *10–15 minutes*

The teacher uses some of the questions and discussion points given, stimulating the children to talk about the story/theme. Some of the questions could be integrated into the reading of the story.

5 The learning activity   *20–35 minutes*

Drama/role play which involves dialling 999.
Some suggested activities could be used in subsequent, follow-up lessons.

| Total time | *45–75 minutes* |

1 INTRODUCE THE THEME

Key points

● Love is a fundamentally important emotion – linking to much else we value. Care, compassion, empathy, courage, etc.

● We should act lovingly (with kindness and care) even when we don't feel loving (though this is harder).

● Being loved helps us to grow into self-confident and loving adults. Being loved and being loving helps us to feel good about ourselves.

● Many people, of all religions, believe that the Divine Being (God) loves us all. Certainly we are *all* valuable and worthy of love.

2 VOCABULARY

Use your usual methods for introducing new words.

The difficult words in the story are:

love	-	*caring deeply, benevolence*
anticipation	-	*expecting something in the future*
urgently	-	*needing attention at once*
frowned	-	*made facial expression of concentration or displeasure*
peered	-	*looking intently*
determined	-	*with strong will*
siren	-	*device that produces the sound an ambulance makes*
frightened	-	*scared*
frail	-	*delicate, weak*
distressed	-	*very upset*
concerned	-	*involved caringly, interested*
interpreter	-	*person who translates between languages*

3 THE STORY:

Flashing Blue Light

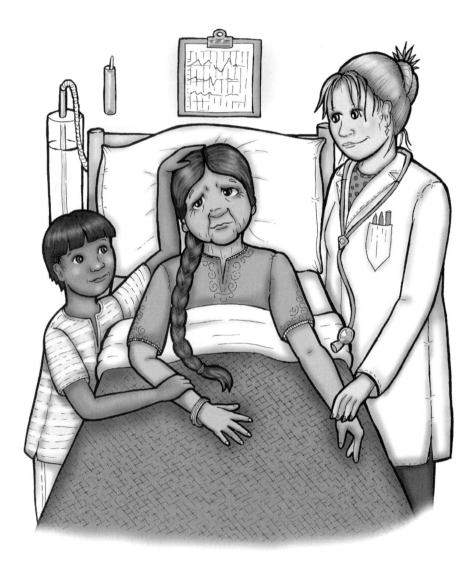

Ranjit loved his grandma and was distressed and brave for her sake

Flashing Blue Light

It was home time. Smiling with anticipation Ranjit ran out of the dark classroom and into the bright sunshine expecting to find his grandma who was always there to meet him. But that day, grandma wasn't there.

"You'll just have to wait for her," said Mrs Watts, his teacher.

"But Miss," said Ranjit, "grandma's never late. Something must be wrong."

Ranjit spoke urgently, for he was very worried.

Mrs Watts frowned. She knew that what Ranjit had said was true. His grandma was always early and waiting, even in the rain.

"We only live round the corner, Miss," Ranjit said. "I'll go and find her."

"We'll look together," Mrs Watts said. Taking Ranjit's hand she hurried towards his house.

No one answered the door. Ranjit peered through the front window and his heart gave a jump. He could see his grandma stretched out on the floor. Before Mrs Watts could stop him, Ranjit climbed onto the window ledge, reached through a small open window at the top, opened the larger window below and climbed in. He ran to his grandma. Her eyes fluttered and she tried to speak. She looked very ill.

"Open the front door, Ranjit," called Mrs Watts.

"Don't worry grandma," Ranjit said, stroking her hair, "my teacher's here." He ran and opened the door for Mrs Watts. The teacher phoned for an ambulance immediately. It came very quickly, to take grandma to the hospital.

"Ranjit, I think you had better come home with me, and we'll phone your mum."

"No," said Ranjit, who had never said 'no' to a teacher before. "I must go with grandma to the hospital," and before Mrs Watts could disagree, he followed the ambulance men, who had put grandma onto a stretcher and was now lifting her into the ambulance. Ranjit followed and sat by her side. He took her hand. He was determined not to leave her.

Mrs Watts and the ambulance men were standing outside the ambulance looking in.

"Grandma doesn't speak English," Ranjit told them. "She's frightened. I have to go with her. Please."

Mrs Watts nodded.

"I would go with him," she said to the ambulance men, "but I have to get back for my own children. Under the circumstances, perhaps he should go with his grandma."

The ambulance men also nodded their agreement and Mrs Watts turned to Ranjit.

"I'll telephone your mum," she promised him. "She'll go straight to the hospital I'm sure."

One of the ambulance men shut the doors. When they drove away, Ranjit could hear the siren wailing, telling all the other cars to make way. He knew that the blue light would be flashing too.

Ranjit knew that he would never forget that ride in the ambulance. He stroked grandma's hand and spoke softly to her in Punjabi.

"Don't worry grandma. You'll be OK. I won't leave you."

Holding tightly onto his hand, she gazed at him with frightened eyes. She looked frail and ill and he could tell that she was in pain. Ranjit loved his grandma and was distressed to see her in pain and fear. He thought of her stories about when she was a little girl in India. She had told him how sad she had been when her own grandma had died.

"Please don't die grandma," he said to himself, and gently, he stroked her hand.

At the hospital doors grandma was put onto a trolley and wheeled in. She was pushed down a long corridor. Ranjit ran by her side. They went into a big lift and, as it moved upwards, grandma moaned. She looked even more frightened than before.

"I'm here grandma. Don't worry. You'll soon be all right."

He was so concerned to comfort her that he had no space in his mind to be frightened himself, though later he was amazed that he had gone into that large, strange place, without his mum and dad, and had not been scared.

The doctor who came to see grandma couldn't speak Punjabi so Ranjit was her interpreter. Even though Ranjit was only eight, he could speak both Punjabi and English very well.

Grandma told Ranjit how she had felt dizzy and had fainted and Ranjit told the doctor.

Photocopiable
Resource

The Story

"Ask her if she has any pain anywhere," the doctor said.

In this way the doctor soon knew just what injection to give to grandma, and by the time Ranjit's mother hurried into their little room, grandma was fast asleep and already looking much better. Ranjit sprang into his mum's arms. He was very happy to see her.

"Grandma's OK mum," he said, as she gave him a big hug.

"Thanks to Ranjit," said the doctor, coming in just at that moment. "Thanks to Ranjit we were able to treat her immediately, and she'll soon be fine. He's a grand lad," she added, rumpling Ranjit's hair. "Brave and kind."

"I know," said Ranjit's mum, and she sounded very proud.

4 TALKING ABOUT THE STORY

Did the children understand?

- How did Ranjit get into grandma's house?

- How did Miss Watts summon the ambulance?

- What did Ranjit do in the ambulance?

- Why did the doctor say Ranjit was brave and kind?

Points for discussion

- **Being loving**
  This is the opportunity to explore the developmental and moral importance of love. The story can be used to show how love brings the best out in us – as it did in Ranjit.

- **Forms of love**
  Discuss the different kinds of love – parental, friendship, neighbourly, religious, romantic, cross-species, etc.

- This is also an opportunity to discuss what to do in an emergency and when/how to dial 999.

5 THE LEARNING ACTIVITY

Links

i)   The activity links to the story through the focus on helping in an emergency and dialling 999.

ii) The assembly connects with the story through the value of love and of helpfulness.

iii) If you wish to link the activity with the assembly, select one of the role plays to be enacted (as well as or in place of the poem or song).

ACTIVITY SUGGESTIONS

- These activities involve working in groups.

- The children will need toy/play telephones.

The teacher will give examples of when we might dial 999.

We want to *help* in an emergency and to summon more *help*.

Divide the class into three groups. Each group will work out a story about an emergency which requires someone to dial 999 (a) for an ambulance (b) for the police and (c) for a fire engine.

The children will take the various roles, described below, required to enact the story.

(a) A road accident

1   The people in a road accident.
2   The person who dials 999 on their mobile.
3   The 999 operator who asks which service they require (ambulance).
4   The ambulance men and women.
5   The people at the hospital.

(b) A fire in a house

1   The people running from the house.
2   The first one out runs to the house next door and uses the telephone to dial 999.
3   The telephone operator who asks which service they require (fire engine and ambulance).
4   The fire men and women.
5   The person who is trapped in the house and rescued.
6   The ambulance men and women.

(c) A bank robbery

1   The people in the bank – customers and bank clerks.
2   The two or three bank robbers who rob and leave.
3   The one who dials 999.
4   The operator who asks what service they require (police).
5   The police men and women who arrive and perhaps drive after and capture the robbers.

Assembly

Theme: Love and Helpfulness

Introduction

The assembly leader introduces the theme and talks about the importance of love and its various forms and how love makes us brave and helpful – as in the story. Goodness and love are like identical twins.

Story

Assembly leader:

"Our story today is about a boy whose love for his grandma helps him to be brave, strong, sensible and caring."

The assembly leader reads the story – *Flashing Blue Light*.

Poem or song

You can choose a poem or a song or both, or the children could enact role plays. Select poems and songs which are relevant to the theme or which echo the story in some way.

Examples

Poems:

Grandma Mabel (love at tea-time)
Page 44 in *Smile Please* by Tony Bradman, published by Puffin, 1989.

Paws (practical love)
Page 115 in *A Very First Poetry Book* by Stanley Cook, published by Oxford University Press, 1984.

Songs:

Magic Penny (reflects the nature of love)
No. 10 in *Alleluya*, published by A&C Black, 1980.

Father, We Thank You for the Night (the value of love)
No. 1 in *Someone's Singing Lord* (2nd Edition), published by A&C Black, 2002.

Would you Turn your Back (strong, compassionate love)
No. 34 in *Every Colour Under the Sun*, published by Ward Lock Educational Co. Ltd., 1983.

Quiet reflection or prayer

For a universal, humanistic or multi-faith assembly:

Quiet reflection

The assembly leader says:
"Think about those who love you and how they help you and be grateful for this love. (Pause) Think how the good things in the world, like helpfulness, care and courage, flow from love and the bad things, like fighting, war and hurting people, flow from hate. (Pause) Think of people in the community who help us. Doctors. Ambulance people. Fire fighters. The police. (Pause) Let us try to be as loving, this day and every day, as we possibly can." (Pause)

Or for Christian schools:

Prayer

Let us pray.

Almighty God,
The God of Love, fill our hearts and minds with love that we will be good and caring people. Help us to act lovingly, even to people we don't like, showing your love in our lives.

Amen.

Chapter 14

Playing Fair

Teacher's Notes

Theme Fourteen: The value of **Justice/Fairness**

Values Education: Learning to be fair is part of **Moral Education**

> Justice is central to morality. Though it is a highly abstract principle, the experience of unfairness is familiar to children and can help them to understand the meaning and value of justice.

Lesson Plan

This five-part lesson plan is only a guide. Teachers are likely to add to or amend the learning activities which are suggested and may sometimes wish to substitute their own. For any part of the session they may wish to allow more or less time than that suggested.

1 Introduce the theme   *5–10 minutes*

What is **justice/fairness**?
The teacher gives examples and explains why we should be fair.
The children add some examples of their own and talk about these.

2 Vocabulary   *5 minutes*

The teacher ensures that the children understand the words given.
This can be integrated into the reading of the story.

3 The story   *5–10 minutes*

The teacher shows the illustration and reads the story.

4 Talking about the story   *10–15 minutes*

The teacher uses some of the questions and discussion points
given, stimulating the children to talk about the story/theme.
Some of the questions could be integrated into the reading of the
story.

5 The learning activity   *20–35 minutes*

To label a world map with all the countries from which the families of
the children in the stories in this book originated. Some suggested
activities could be used in subsequent, follow-up lessons.

| **Total time** | *45–75 minutes* |

1 INTRODUCE THE THEME

Key points

Children often have a strong 'it's not fair' reaction which can help them to understand the notion of justice/fairness. What things have happened which they found unfair?

We don't like people to be unfair to us. It is wrong to be unfair to others.

The notion of equality overlaps but is distinct from fairness.

Give examples of fairness and unfairness such as sharing out sweets equally; not being blamed for something you didn't do; a big child picking on a small child. The children add more examples, and talk about these.

2 VOCABULARY

Use your usual methods for introducing new words.

The difficult words in the story are:

justice/fairness	-	*balanced, right, equal treatment*
puzzle	-	*a fun test to work out*
disappointment	-	*unfulfilled hope*
frustration	-	*strong dissatisfaction felt when prevented from doing something*
perfect	-	*unblemished, complete, correct, excellent*
solved	-	*worked out*
punished	-	*payed back for doing a wrong thing*
interrupt	-	*butt in*
apologise	-	*say sorry for some wrong doing or mistake*
seething	-	*boiling with anger*
embarrassed	-	*ashamed, confused, self-conscious*
stubbornly	-	*without budging or changing one's mind*
spoiled	-	*damaged/marred*
own up	-	*confess*
defending	-	*sticking up for*
repeated	-	*said again*
timid	-	*shy*

3 THE STORY:

Playing Fair

Harry learns several things about being fair

Playing Fair

Harry, his sister Charlotte and their little cousin Louisa had been trying to solve the puzzle for ages and ages. Now they were almost there! But as Harry placed the last bit into the one remaining gap, to his disappointment he saw that, once again, it didn't quite fit.

"Damn," he said.

"You're not supposed to say that," said Louisa.

Harry grinned.

"Miss goody-two-shoes," he joked, pointing at her new sandals. The children laughed, happy to release some of their frustration. The puzzle was a bit like a jigsaw, but it had no picture and even some of the pieces that went on the inside had straight edges. You had to try to make a perfect square, and up to now, however hard they tried, there was always one rounded bit of one jigsaw piece which stuck out from one of the sides.

"We could tear it off," Louisa suggested, pleased by her idea.

"No point," said Charlotte. "We wouldn't have solved the puzzle."

Charlotte was eight and already had grown-up braids in her hair. She was one year older than her brother.

"Louisa doesn't really understand that," Harry thought. "Perhaps she's too young. I give up anyway," he said.

"Me too," said Louisa.

"If we hadn't seen Uncle Gilroy do it right," said Charlotte, "I would think it couldn't be done."

"He goes home tomorrow," said Louisa.

Uncle Gilroy was on a visit from Jamaica and was staying at Louisa's house.

"He'll be taking the puzzle back," said Harry. "We'll not solve it now".

"Not this time anyway," said Charlotte. "Though I think I'll have one last try."

Later Harry and Louisa and their mothers were having tea with Uncle Gilroy. Charlotte wasn't there. She was at her friend's house.

The Story

"You know sometin' children," said Uncle Gilroy, "you surprise me. Spoilin' up me puzzle. De children dem back 'ome like fe try it too you know."

"Spoiling the puzzle Gill?" asked Harry's mum.

Uncle Gilroy held up a torn-off rounded bit.

"Did you do that Harry?" his mum asked.

"No," said Harry, "it wasn't me."

"I think Charlotte was playing with it last," said Louisa's mum.

"Well I am surprised at her," Harry's mum sounded very upset. "I'm so sorry Gill. She'll have to buy you another one."

"You can't buy dem no more you know, but no worry 'bout it Cissy. What done is done," said Uncle Gilroy.

Harry remembered Louisa's words about tearing the puzzle. He looked at her. She looked away. His mum was still talking to Uncle Gilroy.

"Well you can be sure that Charlotte will be punished for …"

"She may not have done it," Harry said.

"Don't interrupt," said his mum. "It's rude, Harry. Apologise this minute."

"But you don't know until you ask her. She wouldn't …" He didn't finish the sentence. This time it was his mum who interrupted.

"Right Harry. Up to your room this minute," she said, in a quiet, angry voice. Louisa looked quite scared.

Harry stormed off. He felt angry too. Once in his bedroom he sat on his bed, seething with anger. How dare she blame his sister without even asking? It wasn't fair! But slowly, as he calmed down, Harry remembered how upset his mum had looked. How upset and embarrassed. He felt his anger shift to Louisa. He was sure that she had solved the puzzle, to her own satisfaction, by tearing off the one bit that each time stubbornly spoiled the square. It was only Louisa who thought you could solve it like that. Yet she hadn't owned up! She had let Charlotte take the blame. That wasn't fair either!

Later his mum came up to his room.

"I'm surprised at you," she said, "defending your sister for such a thing!"

"No! I really don't think she did it mum." He told her about what Louisa had said and he repeated Charlotte's reply. " 'We wouldn't have solved the puzzle.' So you see mum, Charlotte knows you haven't done it right by tearing it, but Louisa doesn't understand. She would just be happy to make the square."

"Oh my," said his mum. "Well at least she defended you. She said you were only sticking up for your sister."

"Well she should have owned up," said Harry. "It's not fair."

"Yes, if she did it, she should. But let's not jump to conclusions. That's not being fair either. And it's exactly what I did, and I'm truly sorry." She gave Harry a hug.

"OK," said Harry. "But whoever did it, I'm pretty sure Charlotte didn't."

"I think you're right Harry. I'll check when she comes home. We can write to Uncle Gilroy later. But remember, Louisa's only young and rather timid. She was actually being brave to stick up for you."

"OK," Harry said again. He smiled. He felt much better.

"Anyway, they've all gone home now. Come down, son, and finish your tea."

4 TALKING ABOUT THE STORY

Did the children understand?

- What shape did you have to make to solve the puzzle?

- Why would Louisa's idea not really solve the puzzle?

- Where did Uncle Gilroy live?

- Who did the grown-ups think had torn the puzzle?

- Who had probably torn it really?

Points for discussion

- Identify all the forms of fairness/unfairness in the story:
  (i)   Harry's mum blaming Charlotte without proof. (We are innocent until proved guilty!)
  (ii) Harry being sent upstairs for rightly defending Charlotte.
  (iii) Louisa not owning up if she had done it.
  (iv) Harry assuming it is Louisa without knowing it.

- Discuss more examples, from the children, of what is fair and unfair.

5 THE LEARNING ACTIVITY

Links

(i)   The activity links to the story through the focus on geography – introduced by Uncle Gilroy coming from Jamaica, and the opportunity to talk about the roots (and unfairness) of racism.

(ii) The story connects to the assembly through valuing justice/fairness.

(iii) If you wish to link the activity to the assembly you could incorporate some of the children's examples of fair/unfair into the assembly talk/introduction, and/or have a labelled world map in the assembly room. You could also have a 'multicultural display' (e.g. positive pictures of people from around the world) as part of the anti-prejudice aspect of fairness.

ACTIVITY SUGGESTIONS

- These activities involve working as a class.
- The children will need: photocopied maps, pens.

1 MAPWORK

Photocopy the map for each child.

Go through the stories.

Where did Carmen come from?	(England)
Where did Maosen and Jie come from?	(China)
Where did Menaka's family come from?	(India)
Where did David come from?	(Perhaps Wales)
Where did Ranjit's grandmother come from?	(India)
Where did Uncle Gilroy come from?	(Jamaica)

On the map, help the children to label England, Wales, Ireland, China, Pakistan, India, the Caribbean (including Jamaica), Japan and Africa.

2 A MULTICULTURAL SOCIETY

Talk to the children about the variety of countries that people have come from to the UK. Inside a simple, outline map of the UK the children draw faces of people from four or five different countries. Help them to colour the skin tones correctly.

You can explain that now, with all these different people, we are a multicultural society with lots of kinds of food, dress, art and music.

Assembly

Theme: Justice/Fairness

Introduction

The assembly leader introduces the theme and talks about the importance of justice and fairness. The children's own examples of fairness/unfairness could be used. The unfairness of prejudice/racism could be explained.

Story

Assembly leader:

"Our story today tell us about various ways in which we are sometimes unfair."

The assembly leader reads the story – *Playing Fair*.

Poem or song

You can choose a poem or a song or both. Select poems and songs which are relevant to the theme or which echo the story in some way.

Examples

Poems:

Complaint (teacher unfairness!)
Page 32 in *Please Mrs Butler* by Allan Ahlberg, published by Puffin, 1984.

You Were the Mother Last Time (taking turns is fair)
Page 16 in *A Very First Poetry Book* by Mary Ann Hoberman, published by Oxford University Press, 1984.

Songs:

Who Can See the Great Wind Blow? (strength to fight wrong)
No. 52 in *Someone's Singing Lord* (2nd Edition), published by A&C Black, 2002.

If I Had a Hammer (value of justice, freedom, love)
No. 40 in Every Colour Under the Sun, published by Ward Lock Educational Co. Ltd., 1983.

Quiet reflection or prayer

For a universal, humanistic or multi-faith assembly:

Quiet reflection

The assembly leader says:
"We admire people who act fairly and we dislike unfairness – against ourselves and against others. Let us quietly think about why we feel like that. (Pause) Sometimes it is hard to know what is fair and to act fairly. Let us promise ourselves that we will try. (Pause) We

will try not to feel or act with prejudice or bullying against people who are different from ourselves. (Pause)

Or for Christian schools:

Prayer

Let us pray.

Dear God,
We praise you as a Just God. Help us to know what is fair and always to have the courage to act fairly. Help us to act without prejudice and without bullying and to respect all human beings, all of whom are your children, from all parts of your world.

Amen.

Chapter 15

Oceans of Wonder

Teacher's Notes

Theme Fifteen: The value of **Wonder** and **Awe**

Values Education: Experiencing wonder and awe is a valuable part of **Spirtual Education**

> **The child's natural feeling of wonder at things should be nurtured and encouraged. If strongly developed it will withstand the utility of the adult world of work and responsibility, to the lifelong enrichment of their spiritual lives.**

Lesson Plan

This five-part lesson plan is only a guide. Teachers are likely to add to or amend the learning activities which are suggested and may sometimes wish to substitute their own. For any part of the session they may wish to allow more or less time than that suggested.

1 Introduce the theme *5–10 minutes*

What is '**wonder**' and '**awe**'?
The teacher gives examples, such as wonder at the stars in the sky, the beauty of a sunset, the birth of a new baby.
The children add some examples of their own and talk about these.

2 Vocabulary *5 minutes*

The teacher ensures that the children understand the words given.
This can be integrated into the reading of the story.

3 The story *5–10 minutes*

The teacher shows the illustration and reads the story.

4 Talking about the story *10–15 minutes*

The teacher uses some of the questions and discussion points given, stimulating the children to talk about the story/theme.
Some of the questions could be integrated into the reading of the story.

5 The learning activity *20–35 minutes*

A painting, collage or poem.
Some suggested activities could be used in subsequent, follow-up lessons.

Total time *45–75 minutes*

1 INTRODUCE THE THEME

Key points

The concept of wonder is to be understood in the spiritual sense (as synonymous with awe rather than with a milder surprise or curiosity).

The teacher seeks to enable the children to understand that wonder and awe involve feeling overwhelmed with amazement and gratitude for some extraordinary or beautiful aspect of creation, and for the fact of creation.

The teacher gives examples, such as the vastness of space and the delicate colours and patterns on a tiny sea-shell.

The children add some examples of their own and talk about these.

2 VOCABULARY

Use your usual methods for introducing new words.

The difficult words in the story are:

wonder and awe	-	*overwhelming amazement and reverence at some aspect of creation*
lagoon	-	*small (saltwater) lake*
enchanted	-	*spellbound*
jagged	-	*having a series of uneven sharp points or spikes*
towering	-	*rising up high above you*
plunge	-	*a sudden drop – often into water*
current	-	*strong movement of water/sea*
aquarium	-	*place for keeping fish*

3 THE STORY:

Oceans of Wonder

Jade discovers the feeling of wonder

Oceans of Wonder

It was the first day of their holiday and identical twins, Jade and Amber, were very excited, though as usual, Jade was playing it cool.

"Mum, can we …" she said, slowly.

"Go to the sea," Amber jumped in, eagerly.

"For a swim perhaps," said Jade.

"Oh yes!" said Amber. "Please."

Amber and Jade often shared out their words.

"Sure," said mum. "We're going to The Blue Lagoon."

"The Blue Lagoon!" said Amber. "That sounds like an enchanted lake in a far-away land."

"Well," said dad, "it's not far at all, but it's pretty good. A kind of huge basin of water in the cliffs. So – into the car everyone. Seaside here we come. Let's see who spots it first."

On the short drive to the beach it was Jade who caught sight of the sea.

"There dad," she yelled, excited in spite of herself. She pointed and Amber saw it too – blue between distant green hills. Soon after this dad parked by the sea and led the way up a steep hill, which brought them to a swaying bridge. They walked across in single file. Amber looked down over a dizzying drop to the jagged rocks below. She clutched the handrail tightly as she felt the bridge wobble under her feet. "Scary!" she thought, surprised to see Jade walking over unconcerned, her hands in her pockets. Amber was the last to reach the other side and she stepped onto the firm pathway with relief. They followed the path as it curved round the hill until suddenly, there it was below them, The Blue Lagoon, a green-blue circle of water, surrounded by towering grey cliffs.

"Wow," said Amber. "It's turquoise. What a wicked place."

They walked down a steep path to a small, stony beach near the water; water which turned out to be freezing cold. The twins crept in, bit by bit, up to their knees.

"You have to take the plunge," Jade told Amber. "Then it's OK."

Amber watched Jade plunge in, right up to her neck, causing the water to surge over Amber who shivered. It was almost painful. Jade had turned and was grinning at her.

"Come on. It's great once you're in. Honest."

Taking a deep breath Amber followed. Jade was right. Suddenly the cold went away. The water felt fine. The twins were strong swimmers. Together they swam right across The Blue Lagoon. At the far side they found a kind of passage between the cliffs where the sea came in. It was harder to swim now, with the current swelling against them, but Amber saw Jade pull herself up onto the cliffs at one side of the opening, and making a big effort, she followed.

"Let's go through the passage," Jade shouted.

Finding a sort of ledge for her feet Amber inched along, following her twin. It was worth the effort. After a few yards the passageway opened out to the bright and beautiful blue sea, which spread out before them, vast and sparkling.

Amber gazed, wide eyed. She felt awed by the power of this endless bright blueness, this vast beauty, presented to them like a precious gift. For several minutes she gazed until her sister's voice broke the spell.

"Look Amber," Jade said. Her voice was full of pleasure. Just a few yards in front of them a seal's head had emerged from the sea. The seal had big, liquid black eyes in a pointed, whiskery face and he was staring at them, curiously. After a moment he slipped back into the water and was gone.

The girls watched and waited but when the seal didn't return they too slipped into the water and let the current carry them effortlessly back into the lagoon.

After their swim, the family had a picnic lunch on the beach. Amber was very hungry.

"Guess what mum," she said. "We went and saw the sea and …"

"and a seal came and, like, saw us," said Jade, her mouth full of sandwich.

"Wasn't it awesome Jade?" Amber said. "Finding the sea like that and the seal and everything."

"The seal was nice," said Jade. "I wouldn't say 'awesome' though."

"Oh you," said Amber. "What would you have to see to say, 'Wow, this is just amazing'?"

Jade thought for a moment.

"Something like it was from another world or something."
She grinned, "and then I'd eat my hat," she said, using one of her
grandmother's old sayings, "'cos I never will!"

"You never know," said Amber.

"That's one way Jade is different from you, Amber," said
mum. "She doesn't find things so magical."

"Magical! Huh," said Jade scornfully. "I really would eat my
hat if I saw something magical."

After lunch they all drove to the Ocean Aquarium. The twins
enjoyed this enormously. The fish were beautiful.

"Look at that one," they kept saying. "Look Amber," and
"look Jade," whenever they saw a particularly unusual kind. But it
was at the very last tank that Amber saw Jade's face change. Jade
was in the lead and came to the tank first. Her eyes widened
and Amber saw that she was holding her breath.

"Look Amber," Jade whispered.

Amber looked. It was a tank full of seahorses. They were
exquisite – from the top of their horse-shaped heads to the tips
of their curly tails.

"Their eyes are like stars," Amber said, noticing their spiky
lashes.

"I thought seahorses were only in fairytales," said Jade, her
voice full of wonder. "Like magic. I never knew they were in the
real ocean. Aren't they just ... totally amazing."

Amber grinned. She took off her sun hat and held it out to
her sister. Mum and dad laughed. Suddenly Jade remembered
what she had said. She pretended to chomp a big bite out of the
hat and made everyone laugh again.

"Well," said mum, "time for home. Even Jade has had a wonderful day."

4 TALKING ABOUT THE STORY

Did the children understand?

- What scared Amber on the bridge?

- What was the name of the place where the twins swam?

- What did they see in the blue sea?

- What did Jade say she would have to see to be amazed?

- What did Jade see that did amaze her?

Points for discussion

- **Wonder**
  Why does Amber feel wonder as she gazes at the sea?
  (Its power, size, beauty. Presented suddenly like a precious gift.)
  Why does Jade feel wonder as she gazes at the seahorses?
  (Their beauty, their other-world fairytale quality.)
  Ask the children what has given them this feeling of wonder.

- **Persons**
  In addition, you could discuss what it is to be a person – thinking about identical twins – identical in looks but different in personality – each a *different person*. The opportunity to talk about the uniqueness of each one of us. We can also feel a sense of wonder/awe at our own existence.

5 THE LEARNING ACTIVITY

Links

i)   The activity links to the story through a focus on the seaside – often a magical place to children.

ii) The assembly connects with the story through valuing wonder and awe – the existence and beauty of the world/universe. (As in theme ten with the story: *The Secret Place*).

iii) If you wish to link the activity with the story, you can do this in two ways:

(a) Display the seaside collage.
(b) The assembly poem. One or more of the children can read their own seaside poem.

ACTIVITY SUGGESTIONS

- These activities involve working as a class and as individuals.

- The children need paints, safe scissors, glue.

1 SEASIDE BRAINSTORM

Make a list, with the children, of all the things you can see at the seaside – the children should suggest most of these (boats, sandcastles, shells, jellyfish, etc.).

2 A CLASS COLLAGE

Each child should choose one of these seaside objects to draw and colour. The children cut out their drawings and stick them onto one large, class, seaside collage.

3 A SEASIDE POEM

(Older) children can write a poem about the seaside. (About 'a seaside holiday', or 'what I do at the seaside' or 'why I like the seaside…'.) Children who have never been to the seaside can write about what they would like to see there.

Assembly

Theme: Wonder and Awe

Introduction

The assembly leader introduces the theme and talks about our wonder and awe at creation and at the beauty of the natural world. Talk about the vastness of the universe and the mystery of life.

Assembly leader:

"Our story today is about twin girls, Jade and Amber. Amber is blessed with the gift of wonder but Jade discovers that she, too, can experience awe."

Story

The assembly leader reads the story – *Oceans of Wonder*.

Poem or song

You can choose a poem or a song or both or the children could read their seaside poems. Select poems and songs which are relevant to the theme or which echo the story in some way.

Examples

Poems:

At the Seaside (celebrates a day at the seaside)
Page 76 in *Smile Please* by Tony Bradman, published by Puffin, 1989.

The Sea or Sea Song (the wonder of the sea and of sea-shells)
Pages 68 and 69 in *A Very First Poetry Book* by John Kitching and James Kirkup, published by Oxford University Press, 1984.

Songs:

Over the Earth is a Mat of Green (the wonder of the world and its loving creator)
No. 10 in *Someone's Singing Lord* (2nd Edition), published by A&C Black, 2002.

Stand Up, Clap Hands, Shout Thank You Lord (a wonderful world!)
No. 14 in *Someone's Singing Lord* (2nd Edition), published by A&C Black, 2002.

I Wonder (wondering about the world)
No. 12 in *Every Colour Under the Sun*, published by Ward Lock Educational Co. Ltd., 1983.

Quiet reflection or prayer

For a universal, humanistic or multi-faith assembly:

Quiet reflection

The assembly leader says:
"Think with amazement about the large size of the universe – the stars and galaxies and infinite space. (Pause) Think with thankfulness about the beauty of our own blue planet, turning in that space. (Pause) Picture for a few moments, your own favourite place or your own favourite creature." (Pause)

Or for Christian schools:

Prayer

Let us pray.

Almighty God,
Creator of the universe, help us to experience wonder that such a universe exists, and to praise your creation. We give thanks for our life and our world.
Amen.